The Enlisted Soldier's Guide

THE ENLISTED SOLDIER'S GUIDE

1st Edition

Dennis D. Perez
Sergeant Major, U.S. Army, Retired

Stackpole Books

Published by
STACKPOLE BOOKS
Cameron and Kelker Streets
P.O. Box 1831
Harrisburg, PA 17105

All photographs courtesy of U.S. Army.

Printed in the U.S.A.

Library of Congress Cataloging-in-Publication Data

Perez, Dennis D.
    The enlisted soldier's guide.

    Includes index.
    1. United States. Army—Handbooks, manuals, etc.
I. Title.
U113.P47 1986   355'.00973   86-5959
ISBN 0-8117-2042-X

Contents

Foreword   9

Preface   11

Acknowledgments   13

Code of Conduct   15

1 Army Traditions   17

    The Salute   19
    Other Courtesies to Officers   20
    Courtesy to the Flag   22
    The Retreat Ceremony   23
    Bugle Calls   24
    The Army Song   26
    The Soldier's Creed   27

2 Training the Army Way   30

    Enlisted Personnel Management System   32
    Career Management Fields   32
    Initial Entry Training   34
    Noncommissioned Officer Education System   35
    Other Military Training Opportunities   36
    Physical Fitness Training   37

3 The Army Post as a Campus   45

Guidance and Counseling   47
Credit by Examination   47
Correspondence Courses   48
Tuition Assistance   48
Scholarships, Loans, and Grants   49
Loan Repayment Program   49
Veterans Educational Assistance Program   50
New GI Bill   51
Schooling Availability   52

4 Excelling   75

Meeting the Board   75
Promotions   79
Enlisted Evaluation Report   96

5 Moving On   106

Enlisted Personnel Assignment System   106
Exchanging Assignments   109
Assignment of Married Couples   110
Overseas Assignments   112

6 Looking Sharp   129

Grooming   131
The Uniform   133
Selected Individual Uniforms   136
Uniform Accessories   158
Finishing Touches   164

7 Finance   174

Monthly Pay Entitlements   176
Monthly Allowances   180
Reenlistment Bonuses   184
Leave   184
Passes   187
Other Financial Matters   187
Deductions from Your Pay   188

8 The Obvious and Not So Obvious   191

Relief Agencies: Help's Available   192
A Home Away from Home—The USO   193
Special Services   194

Travel Benefits 194
Legal Assistance 194

9 Career Decisions 198

Discharges 199
Pregnancy: The Soldier's Options 199
The Reenlistment Bonus 202
The Army Reserve 203
The Army National Guard 203
Active Duty in Another Capacity 204
ROTC 208
Conclusion 212

Glossary 213
Index 217

Foreword

The Army retains only about half of the first-termers, but then I'm not sure an Army career is truly for everyone. Good soldiers, who play the game well and make the team, sometimes leave the Service for various reasons. Actually, good soldiers who return to civilian life after a successful tour in the Army often become the Army's best unofficial recruiters. What is most unfortunate is that sometimes good soldiers leave the Army simply because they were not informed of the variety of opportunities the Army can provide.

Good leadership, guidance, and training are the means through which the Army strengthens the soldier's personal values, thereby causing our Army to be better prepared to better defend our great nation. These informed soldiers become the team's key players. On the other hand, I've seen many soldiers of all ranks who reach a point where they do not want to learn any more. Such soldiers not only hurt their personal career potential but also weaken the team. Therefore, the Army should thank them for their services and require them to depart honorably.

I think this *Guide* contains the starting point for soldiers who want to make the team and achieve the excellence necessary to be all that they can be, either in the Army or after returning to civilian life.

William A. Connelly
Sergeant Major of the Army, Retired

9

Preface

This *Guide* for junior enlisted soldiers is long overdue. I am especially excited knowing that SGM (Ret.) Denny Perez and Stackpole Books have collaborated on this most important endeavor. Stackpole has been the publishing leader in *Guides* for many years, and their excellence in this area is unsurpassed.

SGM (Ret.) Denny Perez has been a soldier most of his adult life. He has experienced the highs and lows of every enlisted rank. His credibility and reputation are impeccable. Perez knows what it takes to progress up the promotion ladder. His outstanding journalistic skills, coupled with his personal experience as an enlisted soldier and senior NCO, make him especially well qualified to author this book.

I'm convinced you will find this *Guide* informative and productive in meeting your career goals. If you have experienced the apprehensions associated with appearing before a promotion board, I know the information in this book will alleviate that concern.

Perez writes intelligently about such diverse subjects as traditions of the service; career "musts"; opportunities in the civilian sector that are enhanced by your Army experience; how to deal with the problems associated with PCSs; and the benefits available to soldiers. He finishes up with a most impressive discussion of the pros and cons of turning your Service experience into a rewarding career.

In short, I highly recommend this *Guide* for all soldiers in the grade of E-5 and below. You and our Army will be better off for it.

Good reading and good luck.

Robert A. Sullivan
Major General, U.S. Army, Retired

Acknowledgments

I am indebted to many people who have helped in the creation of this book, and most especially to my wife, Cheri, a former Army sergeant, now a research engineer, who has contributed extensive thoughts and labors to this project. The advice and input provided by my fellow NCOs was invaluable. In addition, I am indebted to photographers Michael Bogdanowicz, Debbie Drew, Robert DuQuette, Tom Hager, Steven Infanti, Lisa Mena, and Mike Quinn; and to illustrator Lois Knight.

To each, my sincere thanks.

Dennis D. Perez
Sergeant Major, U.S. Army, Retired

Code of Conduct

For Members of the Armed Forces of the United States

"1. I am an American fighting man. I serve in the forces which guard my country and our way of life. I am prepared to give my life in their defense.

"2. I will never surrender of my own free will. If in command I will never surrender my men while they still have means to resist.

"3. If I am captured I will continue to resist by all means available. I will make every effort to escape and aid others to escape. I will accept neither parole nor special favors from the enemy.

"4. If I become a prisoner of war, I will keep faith with my fellow prisoners. I will give no information or take part in any action which might be harmful to my comrades. If I am senior, I will take command. If not, I will obey the lawful order of those appointed over me and will back them up in every way.

"5. When questioned, should I become a prisoner of war, I am required to give name, rank, service number, and date of birth. I will evade answering further questions to the utmost of my ability. I will make no oral or written statements disloyal to my country and its allies or harmful to their cause.

"6. I will never forget that I am an American fighting man, responsible for my actions, and dedicated to the principles which made my country free. I will trust in my God and in the United States of America."

*   *   *   *   *

The Code, an executive order passed in 1955, provides guidance to soldiers in the event they are captured or become prisoners of war during hostilities. This code for the fighting man provides much more however, — it embodies the pride and self-confidence necessary to be the most effective fighting man. It should be read and adopted by all soldiers.

1

Army Traditions

Today's American soldier serves in the most sophisticated, best-equipped military force in the world. Through their joint efforts, soldiers defend this nation using highly technical weapon systems and fighting vehicles. The challenges and training faced by today's soldier are more demanding than ever before in history. But today's soldier is meeting those challenges.

"Wars may be fought with weapons, but they are won by men," General George S. Patton, Jr., said. He added, "It is the spirit of men who follow . . . that gains the victory." His sentiments echoed those of a former American hero, Gen. George Washington, who credited victory to "men of character activated by principles of honor." The men and women of the United States Army have proven their professional competence in Grenada and throughout the world. Each soldier has reason to be proud of the uniform he wears.*

As team members, American soldiers work together to accomplish their mission. An integral part of the unit as a whole, each soldier must assume the responsibility to build on individual strengths and strive to overcome individual weaknesses. Based on ability, experience, and previous training, each soldier can progressively master more difficult and

---

*Note: Throughout this *Guide*, use of the impersonal pronoun "he" is understood to mean "he or she."

First-Termers' Parade

complex tasks. General Patton summed up the soldier's responsibility by stating, "To be a good soldier a man [or woman] must have discipline, self-respect, pride in his unit and his country, a high sense of duty and obligation to his comrades and to his superiors, and self-confidence born of demonstrated ability."

As a new entrant into the world of the professional soldier, or a "first-termer," you have much to learn. You are just beginning a never-ending process of learning and improving. During your first four years of service, this book will help you move within the increasingly complex military environment with ease and confidence. It will provide you with a ready reference on military expectations, sources of assistance, and the rich traditions of Army history.

Traditions within the Army ranks are strong. They show a pride in the military and a professionalism in the soldier. Many customs date back as far as the Continental Army in the American Revolutionary War. Customs add color and pageantry to the military lifestyle. They foster esprit de corps and a sense of belonging.

Some of the military traditions are based quite simply on common sense. For instance, to show pride in the uniform you should never appear in uniform while under the influence of alcohol. Likewise, you should refrain from criticizing the Army in front of a civilian, and more generally you should guard from speaking disrespectfully about your commanders or supervising NCOs. When in a position of leadership, you should practice these same courtesies toward your subordinates.

When situations occur where you have not fulfilled your military duties and are being corrected for the oversight, the best advice is to follow the military tradition of delivering a response of "No excuse, Sir!"

One long-standing tradition that first-termers frequently find frustrating deals with umbrellas. Female soldiers are authorized to carry umbrellas while in uniform; male soldiers, however, are not.

THE SALUTE

The most common military tradition is the greeting rendered by salute. While many forms of salutes are authorized, depending upon the arms you may be carrying and the situation involved, the most common salute is the hand salute. A sharp, crisp salute shows pride in recognizing the comrade in arms; conversely, a sloppy or halfhearted salute shows a lack of pride and is a poor reflection upon the soldier rendering it.

The hand salute is required whenever you recognize an officer. Exceptions are made when the situation so requires—such as in public transportation (buses, planes, and so on) or in public places (such as theaters), or when the salute would be impractical (at work, when driving a vehicle, or when actively engaged in athletics). Even though saluting an officer is not required by military regulation when both soldier and officer are in civilian clothes, the soldier who renders this courtesy is following long-standing military tradition.

If running, you should slow to a walk before saluting. A greeting is often given with the salute. You should hold the salute until it is returned by the officer. Equally important, you should never turn and walk away to avoid rendering a salute. Never salute while holding objects in your right hand. When in a military formation or parade, salute only on command.

The salute itself should be made in one movement, raising the right arm so that the upper arm is horizontal, and bending the elbow so that the tip of the forefinger touches the forehead slightly to the right of the right eyebrow. The fingers and thumb should be extended, with the fingers "joined" or touching one another. Neither the palm nor the back of the hand should be visible from a front view.

If you wear eyeglasses, the fingertip of your right hand should touch the point on the glasses where the front frame joins the temple or earpiece. When you are wearing a utility cap, a service cap, or a helmet, your fingertip should touch the visor of the headgear.

On some occasions you should salute the officer twice. Specifically, if you salute an officer, and the officer stays in your general vicinity but does not converse directly with you, all military courtesies have been fulfilled. When the officer spends a few moments talking with you, however, you should salute a second time at the end of the conversation. This custom can be considered a preliminary greeting followed by a farewell.

When a military vehicle passes carrying an officer that you recognize, you should render a salute. Likewise, if an official vehicle passes displaying vehicle plates or flags that depict the rank of the passenger, you should salute.

The salute is also used to show respect toward the American flag, when the flag passes or during the retreat ceremony. (See *Courtesy to the Flag* and *The Retreat Ceremony* in this chapter for details.)

The best advice on saluting is to render the salute whenever any doubt exists as to whether the salute is actually required. Rendering the salute is a matter of pride.

OTHER COURTESIES TO OFFICERS

A number of customs and courtesies have evolved as a means of showing respect to senior ranking servicemembers. Most are based on the current notion of the position on the right being the place of honor. The origins of this custom lie in ancient days when men fought with swords. Since most men were right-handed, the left side became the defensive side, to be protected by the subordinate.

Today this courtesy is rendered by having the soldier always walk on the left-hand side of a ranking officer. The same is true for riding in vehicles—the subordinate sits on the left of the superior.

For entering a vehicle or small boat, there are also associate customs. The occupants enter by rank, with the highest ranking entering last and exiting first.

An officer entering a room is also shown special courtesy. The first soldier to recognize the officer calls the other personnel in the room to attention, but the soldier does not salute. A salute is rendered indoors only when the soldier is reporting. Soldiers should remain at attention until the officer gives an "at ease" command. This custom is not adhered to in the work environment, where it would frequently be impractical. If at all practical, however, when an officer not commonly working directly with a soldier is in the work environment and addresses the soldier directly, the soldier should stand.

The Salute
When you are wearing the garrison cap, cold weather cap, or beret, the hand salute is to the forehead—except when wearing glasses. When you are wearing the utility cap, camouflage cap, service cap, or helmet, the salute is to the visor.

Standing at attention is also expected of the soldier when he is talking with an officer. Frequently the officer will instruct the soldier to stand at ease. When the conversation is completed, the soldier should return to attention and salute.

One final recommendation on rendering courtesies to officers. You should regard "requests," "desires," or "wishes" expressed by a commanding officer as orders. Frequently, the intent is the same, but the wording is softened as a courtesy to the subordinate.

COURTESY TO THE FLAG

Honoring the nation's flag is an integral part of military customs and courtesies. The hand salute is rendered to show respect when the flag passes in front of a soldier in uniform. You should initiate the salute when the flag is approaching and is within six paces, and then you should hold the salute until the flag has passed six paces. If you are indoors when the flag passes, do not render the hand salute. If you are walking past a stationary flag, the same six-pace rule applies. In addition you should turn your head in the direction of the flag. Soldiers marching in formation render salute only on command.

A soldier in civilian clothes still honors the flag with a salute, but it is modified to a "civilian salute" with the right hand placed over the heart. If headgear is worn (with civilian clothing) by a male soldier, the headgear is removed with the right hand and held over the heart; if the soldier is a female in civilian clothing wearing headgear, she does not remove it but still places her right hand over her heart.

The national flag should never be dipped low as a means of salute or greeting. The only exception is made for military vessels under specific international courtesies. Organizational flags, including the U.S. Army flag, are dipped lower than the national flag during the playing of the National Anthem, To the Color, or a foreign national anthem.

Out of respect for the flag, you should never use it as part of a costume, on a float, or on a vehicle, unless it is displayed on a staff. No lettering of any kind should ever be added to the flag. When a flag is damaged, soiled, or weathered, it should be burned. No portion of the flag should ever be allowed to touch the ground; if it does, the flag is considered soiled. The tradition of folding the flag should be followed exactly.

Four common sizes exist for the national flag. The garrison flag, flown on special occasions and holidays, measures 20 x 38 feet. The post flag, flown for general use, is 10 x 19 feet. The storm flag, used in inclement weather, is 5 x 9.5 feet. The last size is that of the grave decorating flag, which measures 7 x 11 inches.

In addition to the national flag, we can speak of the national color, the national standard, and the national ensign. The national color, carried by dismount units, is a 3 x 4 foot flag trimmed on three sides by a golden yellow fringe measuring 2.5 inches in width. The national standard is identical to the national color, except that it is carried by a mechanized, motorized, or mounted unit; only the name is different. The national ensign is a naval term designating a flag (of any size) used to indicate the nationality of ship personnel. The term *flag* does not technically refer to colors, standards, or ensigns. Other terms associated with flags are also a part of military tradition. The *hoist* is the width, the *fly* is the length, and the *truck* is the ball at the top of the flag staff. The truck represents "the shot heard around the world," a reference to the first shot of the American Revolutionary War.

Another means of showing respect to the flag is the Pledge of Allegiance, first adopted by Congress in 1942. The tradition surrounding the pledge specifies that it should be said while standing at attention, with the right hand over the heart. The Pledge of Allegiance is normally not recited in military formations or in military ceremonies.

Military customs and traditions govern the raising and lowering of the flag, as well. *Reveille* is the daily military ceremony honoring the flag at the beginning of the day. *Retreat* is the counterpart when the flag is lowered at the end of the day. Reveille is a bugle call, often recorded and played over a public address system on military installations today. The flag is hoisted quickly to the top of the flagpole, beginning on the first note of reveille. Retreat ceremonies, full of traditions, are discussed in the following section.

The flag is sometimes flown at half-staff as a salute to the honored dead. Memorial Day, the last Monday in May, is one occasion when the flag is flown at half-staff from reveille to 1200 hours. A 21-gun salute is then fired before the flag is raised to the top of the staff until retreat. Whenever the flag is to be flown at half-staff, it is first to be hoisted to the top of the staff and then lowered down to the midpoint. Likewise, before lowering the flag, it is to be again hoisted the full height of the staff and then lowered and properly folded.

Full details on flag courtesies can be found in AR 840-10.

THE RETREAT CEREMONY

The purpose of the retreat ceremony is to honor the national flag at the end of the day. Often the *evening gun* is fired at the time of retreat so that soldiers throughout the installation will be aware of the ceremony even if they are outside the range of the bugle. The evening gun also is used to mark the end of the work day.

Retreat is not necessarily at the same time at each installation. The post commander sets the time of the sounding of both reveille and retreat.

During the retreat ceremony, at the last note of retreat the evening gun is fired. At that time either a band, a bugler, or recorded music will be used to play the National Anthem or to sound To the Color. Soldiers will begin lowering the flag on the first note of the National Anthem or To the Color, at a rate that will ensure that the lowering is completed with the last note of music. Then, following strict customs, the flag will be folded and stored until reveille the next morning.

Special respect is rendered to the flag and to the National Anthem during retreat by soldiers all across the installation, not merely by those participating directly in the ceremony. Under no circumstances should the professional soldier run into a building to avoid rendering this courtesy to the flag.

During the playing of the National Anthem, soldiers in uniform should stand at attention, facing the flag if visible, or the music if the flag is not visible. A salute should be rendered on the first note and held until the final note. The same courtesy applies to To the Color. When indoors, the salute is omitted. If in civilian clothing, the soldier renders the "civilian salute," in the same manner as to the flag. Women never remove headgear.

All vehicular traffic should stop during the retreat ceremony. For cars and motorcycles, the driver and passengers should get out of the vehicle and show proper respect. For other vehicles, such as buses or armored vehicles, the ranking soldier should get out and render the appropriate salute. All other passengers should sit quietly at attention inside the vehicle. Commanding officers of tanks or armored cars can salute from the vehicle.

The same respect should be rendered to the national anthems of friendly nations when they are played during official occasions.

BUGLE CALLS

In addition to reveille and retreat, several other bugle calls play important roles in military tradition. In general, bugle calls can be divided into four categories: Alarm, Formation, Service (which includes reveille and retreat), and Warning.

First call is the first bugle of the day. Considered a warning call, it warns you that reveille is about to take place and that you will be late if you're not ready within the next few minutes.

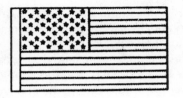

OPEN EDGE

FOLD THE LOWER STRIPED SECTION OF THE FLAG OVER THE BLUE FIELD.

FOLDED EDGE

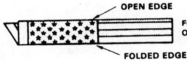

OPEN EDGE

FOLD THE FOLDED EDGE OVER TO MEET THE OPEN EDGE.

FOLDED EDGE

START A TRIANGULAR FOLD BY BRINGING THE STRIPED CORNER OF THE FOLDED EDGE TO THE OPEN EDGE.

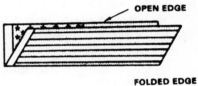

OPEN EDGE

FOLDED EDGE

FOLD THE OUTER POINT INWARD PARALLEL WITH THE OPEN EDGE TO FORM A SECOND TRIANGLE.

CONTINUE FOLDING UNTIL THE ENTIRE LENGTH OF THE FLAG IS FOLDED INTO A TRIANGLE WITH ONLY THE BLUE FIELD AND MARGIN SHOWING.

TUCK THE REMAINING MARGIN INTO THE POCKET FORMED BY THE FOLDS AT THE BLUE FIELD EDGE OF THE FLAG.

THE PROPERLY FOLDED FLAG SHOULD RESEMBLE A COCKED HAT.

Lowering and Folding the U.S. Flag

While the flag of the United States is being lowered from the staff and folded, no part of it should be allowed to touch the ground. The flag should be folded into the shape of a cocked hat.

The last bugle call of the day is *Taps,* a service call dating back to Civil War days. Taps is traditionally used at military funerals, as well, giving the final bugle call for the fallen soldier.

To the Color is the alternate music used during the retreat ceremony. It signals that the flag is being lowered. You should render the salute during To the Color much as you would during the National Anthem. Both are meant to honor the flag.

Tattoo is usually played near 2100 hours and has traditionally been the call for lights out in fifteen minutes.

THE ARMY SONG

Another tradition that literally brings soldiers to their feet is The Army Song. When you hear it being sung or being played, the appropriate action is to stand at attention. The melody is that of the "Caisson Song," composed in the early 1900s by then Lt. Edmund L. Gruber, who later was promoted to brigadier general. But the words for "The Army Goes Rolling Along" were selected much later. The eight-year process began in 1948 with a nationwide contest to create an official Army song. Within four years the Army had also enlisted the aid of several music composers, publishers, and recording studios. Their joint efforts produced the new lyrics, set to the music of the old "Caisson Song." "The Army Goes Rolling Along" became the official Army song when it was dedicated on Veterans Day, 11 November 1956, at Army installations throughout the world.

The Army Goes Rolling Along

Verse:

"March along, sing our song
  With the army of the free.
Count the brave, count the true
  Who have fought to victory.
We're the Army and proud of our name!
We're the Army and proudly proclaim:

1st Chorus:

"First to fight for the right
  And to build the nation's might,
And THE ARMY GOES ROLLING ALONG.
Proud of all we have done,
  Fighting till the battle's won,
And THE ARMY GOES ROLLING ALONG.

Refrain:

"Then it's hi! hi! hey!
  The Army's on its way,
Count off the cadence loud and strong:
For where'er we go, you will always know
That THE ARMY GOES ROLLING ALONG.

2nd Chorus:	"Valley Forge, Custer's ranks,
	   San Juan Hill and Patton's tanks,
	And the Army went rolling along.
	Minutemen from the start,
	   Always fighting from the heart,
	And the Army keeps rolling along.

Refrain:	"Then it's hi! hi! hey! The Army's on its way, Count off the cadence loud and strong: For where'er we go, you will always know That THE ARMY GOES ROLLING ALONG.

3d Chorus:	"Men in rags, men who froze,
	   Still that Army met its foes,
	And the Army went rolling along.
	Faith in God, then we're right
	   And we'll fight with all our might
	As the Army keeps rolling along.

Refrain:	"Then it's hi! hi! hey!
	   The Army's on its way,
	Count off the cadence loud and strong:
	   (two! three!)
	For where'er we go, you will always know
	That THE ARMY GOES ROLLING ALONG!
	   (Keep it rolling!)
	And THE ARMY GOES ROLLING ALONG!"

THE SOLDIER'S CREED

In its long history, the Army has acquired many traditions, customs, and courtesies. One of the relatively younger traditions, which often warms the soldier's spirit and enhances his pride, is "The Soldier's Creed":

"I am an American Soldier. I am a man (woman) of the United States Army—a protector of the greatest nation on earth. Because I am proud of the uniform I wear, I will always act in ways creditable to the military service and the nation it is sworn to guard.

"I am proud of my own organization. I will do all I can to make it the finest unit of the Army. I will be loyal to those under whom I serve. I will do my full part to carry out orders and instructions given me or my unit.

"As a soldier, I realize that I am a member of a time-honored profession—that I am doing my share to perpetuate the principles of freedom for which my country stands. No matter what situation I am in, I will never do anything, for pleasure, profit, or personal safety, which will disgrace my

A Fighting Man

uniform, my unit, or my country. I will use every means I have, even beyond the line of duty, to restrain my Army comrades from actions disgraceful to themselves and the uniform.

"I am proud of my country and its flag. I will try to make the people of this nation proud of the service I represent, for I am an American soldier."

2

Training the Army Way

The Green Machine is doing especially well. The quality of the soldier today is higher than it has ever been. This is due, to a significant degree, to the first-term soldier. Eighty-eight to ninety percent of first-term soldiers are high school graduates. This is significant because Army training has become more arduous, more demanding, and certainly, more challenging. The all-important foundation provided by these soldiers is necessary in order to maintain and continue to improve the climate of quality in today's Army.

Quite necessarily, training and schooling are slowly being tied into promotions to specific levels. For example, as of 1986 the completion of the Primary Leadership Development Course is a requirement for promotion to staff sergeant. Also, there is a comparable requirement for promotions to all NCO grades.

What does this mean to you, the first-termer? If you intend to make a career of the Army, you can expect to be in some phase of formal training within the NCO Education System (NCOES) at least every three to four years. Often training will occur more frequently. Some estimates predict that, throughout a military career, soldiers will spend up to one-third of their time in some sort of technical or leadership training.

Bayonet Practice

Like many soldiers, you may not finalize your career choice early in your first enlistment. A solid foundation in military education and training, however, will provide you with a solid platform from which you may launch a successful career either in the military or after a return to civilian life.

ENLISTED PERSONNEL MANAGEMENT SYSTEM (EPMS)

While on active duty, your opportunity for military training is extensive. The Enlisted Training System is in actuality a subsystem of the Enlisted Personnel Management System. An integrated program combining classification, evaluations, promotions, assignments, and training, EPMS provides you with logical career development.

The Enlisted Training System is arranged in two distinct but closely related phases: Initial Entry Training (IET) and the Noncommissioned Officer Education System (NCOES).

CAREER MANAGEMENT FIELDS (CMF)

From the entry level recruit to the command sergeant major, all enlisted soldiers are grouped into career management fields so that progress and training are provided throughout their careers.

Each CMF is a grouping of related MOSs*. MOSs are grouped so that soldiers in one specialty have the potential abilities and aptitudes for training and assignments in most of the other specialties within that CMF. In this manner, progression and promotions are facilitated by training. Each soldier has a visible, logical career path mapped out in front of him.

As soldiers climb the promotion ladder within a CMF, new recruits fill in the lower rungs of the ladder, preparing themselves for upward mobility as well. The Army has established career paths for each CMF so that the soldier can be adequately counseled on the training and education he will need. The grouping of related MOSs provides enough flexibility so that the soldier can move laterally within a CMF as well.

Within each CMF, the EPMS has identified the necessary skills for successfully functioning at each grade. Soldiers looking toward promotions need to be constantly preparing themselves for the next higher skill level. Skill Level 1 identifies those skills, proficiencies, and abilities typically needed to perform efficiently in grades E3 and E4. Skill Level 2

---

*Military Occupational Specialties. See the Glossary for selected acronyms and abbreviations.

relates to grade E5; Skill Level 3 to E6; Skill Level 4 to E7; and Skill Level 5 to E8 and E9. It should be noted that due to the grouping of MOSs into CMFs, the skills necessary for Skill Level 2 in a particular CMF will not necessarily be the same skills required at that level in a different CMF.

The EPMS has established 32 CMFs for enlisted soldiers.

CMF 11	Infantry
CMF 12	Combat Engineering
CMF 13	Field Artillery
CMF 16	Air Defense Artillery
CMF 18	Special Operations
CMF 19	Armor
CMF 23	Air Defense System Maintenance
CMF 27	Land Combat and Air Defense System Intermediate
CMF 28	Aviation Communications Electronics System Maintenance
CMF 29	Communications—Electronics Maintenance
CMF 31	Communications—Electronics Operations
CMF 33	Electronic Warfare/Intercept System Maintenance
CMF 51	General Engineering
CMF 54	Chemical
CMF 55	Ammunition
CMF 63	Mechanical Maintenance
CMF 64	Transportation
CMF 67	Aircraft Maintenance
CMF 71	Administration
CMF 74	Automatic Data Processing
CMF 76	Supply
CMF 79	Recruitment and Reenlistment
CMF 81	Topographic Engineering
CMF 84	Public Affairs and Audio Visual
CMF 91	Medical
CMF 92	Petroleum
CMF 93	Aviation Operation
CMF 94	Food Service
CMF 95	Law Enforcement
CMF 96	Military Intelligence
CMF 97	Band
CMF 98	Electronic Warfare (EW)/Cryptologic Operations

The 32 CMFs, in turn, are organized into three branches: combat arms, combat support, and combat service support. The Enlisted Training

System recognizes the distinction necessary between branches, but frequently some leadership-type training is possible in the combat support and combat service support branches.

INITIAL ENTRY TRAINING (IET)

Every soldier in the Army has gone through Initial Entry Training, whether or not he was aware of the label applied to the training received. There are two phases of IET: Basic Training (BT) and Advanced Individual Training (AIT), which is MOS training.

Soldiers entering the combat arms branch or the military police MOS receive One Station Unit Training; in other words they remain in the same unit for their Basic Training (BT) and MOS training. Soldiers entering the combat support or combat service support branches generally must change duty assignments for their Advanced Individual Training (AIT), due primarily to the highly technical nature of many of the MOSs in these branches.

The primary functions of IET are to prepare the recruit for military life, provide soldiers with the basic military combat skills, and provide soldiers with Skill Level 1 technical training.

The drill sergeant is a key figure in preparing the recruit for the rigors of Army life. The new soldier must learn the Army system and understand and appreciate how individuals can contribute to the military structure. He must develop self-confidence, self-respect, and self-discipline in order to maximize the opportunities that will be available. Equally important, the drill sergeant must ensure that the new soldier is strong and physically fit.

The basic military combat skills are essential for every soldier, regardless of the branch in which he will serve. Since the main business of the Army is national defense, it is essential that each soldier is fully versed in the basics of combat.

To reinforce the training initiated in Basic Training, all soldiers are given additional training in basic skills during the AIT phase of IET. Field training exercises frequently are used to combine the specialized MOS training the soldier must receive with the basic soldier skills that need to be reinforced. AIT narrows the perspective of IET, though, highlighting those specific skills soldiers will need to perform in their particular CMF at Skill Level 1.

IET provides training at the apprentice level, preparing the soldier to be a contributing member to his unit upon arrival. The training however, is by no means complete. Field units are responsible for providing continuing on-the-job training to round out the soldier's initial training and to enhance the first-termer's potential.

NONCOMMISSIONED OFFICER EDUCATION SYSTEM (NCOES)

The second phase of the Enlisted Training System is NCOES, which has a single goal as its objective—to train NCOs to be trainers and leaders for the soldiers who work under their supervision. Leadership study is crucial, but in today's advanced military environment, technical training is also critical. Therefore, NCOES provides an extensive network of courses at all levels of the NCO corps. NCOES is not limited to a single school or location. It is conducted in service schools and NCO academies (NCOA) within CONUS and overseas as well.

Each of the four levels of training in NCOES focuses on a specific grade or experience level. The primary level training for E5s who hold a leadership position within their squad is provided through the NCOA. The Primary Leadership Development Course (PLDC) is, however, available to all soldiers. It emphasizes leadership skills, preparing the soldier to fulfill such duties. As mentioned earlier, as of 1986 PLDC is a requirement for promotion to E6, the first step in the Army's move toward tying NCOES to promotions. Combat support and combat service support soldiers also receive Primary Technical Courses (PTC) in the first level of NCOES. PTCs, presented in service schools, provide specific Skill Level 2 training needed for the soldier to be effective in the E5 grade.

Basic level training (Skill Level 3) is also divided for the combat arms soldiers and for the combat support or combat service support soldiers. The Basic Noncommissioned Officer Course, presented through the NCOA, is geared toward the soldier filling roles such as the tank commander or the squad leader. Basic Technical Courses provide continuing training for the combat support and combat service support personnel. They are offered through service schools.

The advanced and senior level training, for Skill Levels 4 and 5, continue the combat arms leadership training through NCOA and the technical training for combat support and combat service support through service schools.

Regardless of the branch in which a soldier serves, the capstone of NCO training is the United States Army Sergeants Major Academy (USASMA). Selected senior NCOs are trained for positions of the highest responsibility throughout the Army and the DOD. In addition, a First Sergeants Course and an Intelligence Course are also available through the USASMA for those who qualify at this level of training.

Leadership Reaction Course

OTHER MILITARY TRAINING OPPORTUNITIES

Military educational opportunities are not limited to the NCOES courses. The Army provides a myriad of special programs designed to fit the needs of each soldier.

During basic training, soldiers who have a native language other than English are tested and evaluated on their English comprehension. For those soldiers having difficulty with their second language (English), self-paced instruction is available through the Army education centers. English as a Second Language (*ESL*) courses are presented to the basic trainee. In addition, refresher and sustaining courses are available at most installations worldwide. Once at the permanent duty station, the ESL graduate requests further training through his unit commander. The primary consideration is the soldier's willingness to learn and to use English skills to enhance his productivity and efficiency.

The Army Apprenticeship Program is a unique educational opportunity provided by the Army through the Department of Labor. Under the program a soldier's on-the-job training and experience are documented. Once the servicemember has completed 6,000 to 8,000 hours of training and/or experience (approximately three to four years), he can apply to the Bureau of Apprenticeship and Training of the Department of Labor for a Certificate of Completion at the Journeyworker status in the particular trade or vocation in which he has been serving. The certificate earned through the Army program is identical to one earned through civilian sources. While it can by no means guarantee a job for the soldier if he returns to the civilian community, it will make the soldier eligible for vocations requiring the certification. Basically, it gives the soldier a competitive advantage. Equally important, the apprenticeship program encourages the striving for excellence within the military career field.

Ambitious soldiers striving to excel in their military performance can improve their promotion potential through military education. Many soldiers compete for the space allocations in the NCOES; not all soldiers can be selected at a given time. Soldiers can improve their competitiveness by enrolling in NCOES and other military-related correspondence courses. The First Sergeant or training NCO can provide further information on these courses.

MOS Related Instruction courses are also available through the Army education center on each post. Any soldier may enroll in these programs, which are designed to improve skills and enhance advancement potential.

The Basic Skills Education Program (BSEP) is yet another avenue toward personal and military development. The BSEP courses are organized in two skill levels, each covering the functional job-related skills, such as reading, math, and verbal communications. Entry into BSEP must be approved by the soldier's commander. Operated through the Army education center, BSEP's aim is to bring the soldier's abilities up to the Skill Level 1 and Skill Level 2 standards acceptable in NCOES. With sufficient motivation and hard work, a soldier can overcome most deficiencies.

Similar to BSEP, the Advanced Skills Education Program (ASEP) enhances the career potential of selected NCOs. With the commander's recommendation, an NCO can enroll in ASEP for the purpose of reinforcing managerial, supervisory, and communication skills, all inherent to performing successfully at skill levels 3, 4, and 5.

PHYSICAL FITNESS TRAINING

"Our Armed Forces must be mentally and physically prepared at all times, leaving no doubt about this nation's will and ability to defend itself.

For this reason, it is necessary to reaffirm the importance of physical fitness. Even with today's modern weapon systems it is the serviceman and woman who are physically, mentally, and spiritually ready to serve their country who will make the difference in any future conflict." (President Ronald Reagan)

Whether in Grenada, Vietnam, or CONUS, the individual soldier has a significant influence on his comrades and their joint mission. If one soldier is not "fit to fight," he can have a devastating affect on comrades and on the ultimate outcome of the unit's mission. Consequently, it is essential that the Army's physical fitness program be as comprehensive as possible. It encompasses weight control, diet and nutrition, exercise, and stress management to provide guidance toward the development of a totally fit soldier, one who is "fit to win."

Weight Control

The soldier should look trim and neat, not only through proper care of the uniform but also through proper weight control. The Army places such high priority on weight control that a bar from reenlistment or extension to

Physical Fitness Training

a current enlistment can be enacted against soldiers not meeting minimum Army standards. Involuntary separation from service could also be enacted if a soldier has been unsuccessful in meeting Army weight standards after spending six months in the Army Weight Control Program. In addition, overweight soldiers will not be considered for promotion and will not be authorized to attend professional military or civilian schooling until they have met Army weight standards.

Regulations of the Army Weight Control Program aim to ensure that all soldiers are physically able to perform under the most strenuous (combat) conditions and that all soldiers maintain a trim military appearance.

While all personnel are encouraged to strive for a stringent percentage of body fat (20% for males; 28% for females), a more lenient maximum allowable body fat percentage has been established by age group and sex.

Age Group	Sex	Percentage
17–20	M	20
	F	28
21–27	M	22
	F	30
28–39	M	24
	F	32
40+	M	26
	F	34

In addition to the maximum body fat composition, the Army has established a maximum weight, based on height, age group, and sex.

Height (in.)	Male				Female			
	17–20	21–27	28–39	40+	17–20	21–27	28–39	40+
58	—	—	—	—	104	107	110	113
59	—	—	—	—	107	110	114	117
60	132	136	139	141	111	114	117	121
61	136	140	144	146	115	118	121	125
62	141	144	148	150	119	123	126	130
63	145	149	153	155	123	126	130	134
64	150	154	158	160	126	130	134	138
65	155	159	163	165	130	134	138	142
66	160	163	168	170	135	139	143	147
67	165	169	174	176	139	143	148	151
68	170	174	179	181	143	147	151	156
69	175	179	184	186	147	151	155	160

Height	Male				Female			
(in.)	17–20	21–27	28–39	40+	17–20	21–27	28–39	40+
70	180	185	189	192	151	156	160	165
71	185	189	194	197	155	159	164	169
72	190	195	200	203	160	164	169	174
73	195	200	205	208	165	169	174	179
74	201	206	211	214	170	174	180	185
75	206	212	217	220	175	179	184	190
76	212	217	223	226	180	185	190	196
77	218	223	229	232	184	190	195	201
78	223	229	235	238	189	194	200	206
79	229	235	241	244	194	199	205	211
80	234	240	247	250	198	204	210	216

All personnel must be weighed at the time of the Army Physical Fitness Test or at least every six months. In addition, body fat composition testing is required whenever a supervisor feels that the soldier's appearance suggests excessive body fat. Soldiers who exceed either maximum body fat percentage or maximum weight limits will enter a weight control program that includes nutritional training and exercise programs. These programs are administered by health officials. Weight loss and body fat goals are established, and monthly weigh-ins are required.

Few exceptions are allowed. A commander may approve an extension of enlistment, however, for a soldier with a *temporary* medical condition that precludes weight loss and who is currently under a doctor's care; or for a pregnant soldier, fully qualified for reenlistment except for exceeding weight requirements (a pregnant soldier can be allowed to extend her enlistment until six months after the birth of the child, at which time she must meet minimum standards). Commanders may allow reenlistment for the overweight soldier only if a medically documented condition precludes the soldier from attaining the required standard and a disability separation would not be appropriate.

Diet and Nutrition

The Army's concern about weight control and body fat composition highlights the need for adequate information on proper diet and nutrition. The key to a healthy diet is wide variety of foods, a low percentage of empty calories from "junk foods," only small amounts of fat, sugar, salt, and alcohol, and adequate amounts of starch and fiber. Increased awareness of the importance of nutrition has led to alterations in the food preparation in Army dining halls. New menus incorporate a 25 percent reduction in salt and a reduction in the frequency that fried foods are offered (baked and roasted versions of the same items are featured instead). Other changes include the posting of calories contained in all menu items and the availability of salad bars when at all possible.

Even the order in which foods are presented has come under the scrutiny of Army regulations. To encourage the soldier to make sensible diet choices salads and fresh fruits are presented first, then soups, entrées, hot vegetables, starches, and breads. Desserts, with their high sugar and low nutritional value, are held back until the soldier has had a chance to fill his tray with other choices.

Selecting foods from the basic food groups is a good starting place for a balanced diet. The fruit and vegetable group provides fiber, minerals, and vitamins, especially when fresh selections are made instead of canned or frozen; the raw form is also most nutritious. At least four and as many as nine servings a day should come from this group.

The bread and cereal group provides carbohydrates the body needs as its energy food. Whole grain selections provide significant amounts of fiber, as well as iron and vitamins. At least four servings a day are needed.

Protein rich foods, such as poultry, fish, eggs, and red meats, provide minerals in addition to protein. Beans, peas, soybeans, and lentils are other excellent sources of protein. The American diet overemphasizes meats. Ideally, only two servings a day should be consumed, and then they should be about three ounces each. By that standard, one twelve-ounce steak is a two-day supply of meat.

Dairy foods provide protein, in addition to calcium (especially important to women), phosphorous, and vitamins. Skim milk is recommended over whole milk; two-percent is an acceptable alternative. Yogurt and cheeses add variety to the dairy group. Three servings a day are adequate.

Many books are available commercially that provide nutritional information for the health-conscious and the dieter. Using common sense is the best approach to "dieting," however, and fad diets, or diets that emphasize only one or two food choices, are not sensible.

Exercise

Exercise combined with a sensible diet leads to weight control. All three concepts must be viewed as an integrated package. Even more importantly, all three must be viewed in light of their impact on your overall physical fitness.

A fit soldier is one whose body has cardiorespiratory fitness, muscular fitness, flexibility, and correct body fat composition. Each of these four components of fitness can be strengthened through a sensible exercise program.

Cardiorespiratory fitness is the efficiency with which the body can deliver oxygen and nutrients to the muscles through the blood system. Aerobic exercises increase cardiopulmonary functions. Muscular fitness encompasses muscular strength and muscular endurance. Both forms of muscular functions are enhanced by an efficient cardiorespiratory system. Flexibility is as important as strength and endurance to your overall fitness. The full range of motion in the joints can be enhanced by exercises requiring rotating and stretching.

Working on an exercise program should be a regular, but gradual, process. Any new program should be approached in phases. The preparatory phase conditions both the cardiorespiratory system and the muscular system so that both become accustomed to exercise. In the conditioning phase, you can begin to increase your muscular strength and endurance. For ideal conditioning, workouts should be at least three times a week, with no more than a two-day rest between workouts. Without a maintenance phase you can soon find yourself right back where you started—out of condition. Maintenance should also include at least three workouts a week, but shorter, less intense workouts can be used to maintain fitness.

Individual exercise programs are generally more successful when you use the "buddy system." Not only is there an increased safety factor in case one of you should be hurt during the exercising, but the encouragement of another soldier can keep the program progressing.

Common sense safety rules should be applied, such as using exercise equipment only after proper instructions; wearing appropriate reflective gear when jogging at night; and wearing proper footgear during exercise. Cool-down periods are essential for safe exercise programs. Stretch exercises or walking can be used to allow your body time to slow back down to a "normal" pace after a rigorous workout. Keeping a record of the exercise program is another form of encouragement.

Army Physical Fitness Tests

The Army's increased emphasis on physical fitness is reflected in the revised standards implemented in 1986. Soldiers need to be in a regular exercise program in order to maximize test results. The three events test your endurance, strength, and cardiorespiratory efficiency.

The first event administered is a two-minute push-ups test, which measures the strength and endurance of the chest and shoulder muscles and of the triceps. Any push-ups performed that do not match the correct

PUSH-UP	17-21	Male	42/82
		Female	18/58
	22-26	Male	40/80
		Female	16/56
	27-31	Male	38/78
		Female	15/54
	32-36	Male	33/73
		Female	14/52
	37-41	Male	32/72
		Female	13/48
	42-46	Male	26/66
		Female	12/45
	47-51	Male	22/62
		Female	10/41
	52-Plus	Male	16/56
		Female	9/40

SIT-UP	17-21	Male	52/92
		Female	50/90
	22-26	Male	47/87
		Female	45/85
	27-31	Male	42/82
		Female	40/80
	32-36	Male	38/78
		Female	35/75
	37-41	Male	33/73
		Female	30/70
	42-46	Male	29/69
		Female	27/67
	47-51	Male	27/67
		Female	24/64
	52-Plus	Male	26/66
		Female	22/62

RUN (Min:Sec)	17-21	Male	15:54/11:54
		Female	18:54/14:54
	22-26	Male	16:36/12:36
		Female	19:36/15:36
	27-31	Male	17:58/13:18
		Female	21:00/17:00
	32-36	Male	18:00/14:00
		Female	22:36/18:36
	37-41	Male	18:42/14:42
		Female	23:36/19:36
	42-46	Male	19:12/15:12
		Female	24:00/20:00
	47-51	Male	19:36/15:36
		Female	24:30/20:30
	52-Plus	Male	20:00/16:00
		Female	25:00/21:00

Standards for the Three Events
(Number of repetitions in relationship to age and gender)

form will not be counted. A ten- to twenty-minute rest is allowed before the second event.

Sit-ups, testing the strength of the abdominal and flexor muscles, are the second test. A two-minute test period is allowed for this exercise as well. A holder assists you by holding your feet firmly on the ground during the exercise.

The final event, a two-mile run, measures your aerobic and leg muscle endurance. Walking is discouraged during the running event, but it is not unauthorized. The shorter the time period needed to complete the run, the higher the score.

3

The Army Post as a Campus

Education is an important and integral part of military life. It sharpens skills and abilities and maximizes your potential, affecting your promotions and career development. Educational experiences in the military classroom and on the job are only one small part of the total educational opportunities provided to today's soldier. In fact, at most Army installations you can earn a college degree without ever leaving the post.

According to Secretary of the Army John O. Marsh, Jr., soldiers must "recognize education as a lifelong learning process." He further stated that soldiers should not view their stint in the Army as time lost from the college campus. In fact, Pentagon officials have seriously considered requiring senior NCOs to have a minimum educational requirement of an associate degree or two years of college to be considered for further promotions after their fourteenth or fifteenth year in service. The board reviewing this matter declined to make it a requirement in 1986, but the board did raise the minimum educational requirements for promotion to E5 to high school graduation or GED equivalent. Increasing emphasis on higher education may well mean that you will soon see many of your peers taking off-duty college courses to stay competitive in the promotion arena.

The Army is serious about its commitment to you to provide the best possible educational opportunities. Recently, an awareness campaign began Army-wide, with the slogan "Reaching for Excellence," designed to market programs available through local education centers.

Through Army Education Centers (AEC) located on each post, the Army provides an integrated system of educational courses, spanning from the high school and college preparatory level to post-master's work. Testing, guidance and counseling, and course work, both on- and off-post at both the vocational and college levels, complement your efforts. Whether stationed in the United States or overseas, you have a wide variety of offerings. As a minimum, centers provide resources such as an MOS library, testing services, the Servicemembers' Opportunity Colleges (SOC), career counseling, and skill development programs for language, MOS, and occupationally oriented courses.

In addition, the benefits are not restricted to active duty personnel. Several programs are available to help you pursue your educational goals after returning to civilian life. Other programs aid your spouse and children.

The variety of programs available to you and your dependents would be of little use were it not for the availability of time. A few programs allow you to participate during duty hours. For instance, you can attend certain vocational courses or MOS-related training, as well as language training, when a PCS overseas is scheduled. Most programs, however, involve your off-duty time, during lunchtime, evening, or weekend hours. In addition, the education centers maintain office hours that afford easy access during off-duty time.

Education Center

GUIDANCE AND COUNSELING

The Army is committed to education, but more importantly, it is committed to the development of the individual soldier. Your goals and aspirations may vary widely from those of other soldiers. The Army Continuing Education System (ACES) can help you reach your personal educational goals.

Professional guidance counselors at each education center help you identify both long- and short-range educational goals. (You are required to attend counseling sessions at the AEC within 30 days of assignment to a new post.) The counselors have diagnostic tests and interest inventories to help you analyze your aptitudes and interests. They can also provide the most current information on the educational programs available at your new duty station.

CREDIT BY EXAMINATION

In addition to nationally recognized achievement tests needed for entrance into some colleges, such as the Scholastic Aptitude Test (SAT) and the American College Testing (ACT) program, ACES provides a variety of testing programs through which you can receive college credit without ever entering the classroom.

The Defense Activity for Nontraditional Education Support (DANTES) is one such program. DANTES offers the means by which you can receive college credit for knowledge acquired through experience, personal reading, or independent study. DANTES also offers self-study courses to help you prepare for tests you may wish to challenge. You are not required to pay for any DANTES tests, but your dependents must pay a nominal fee.

Two types of testing programs are available through DANTES. First, the College Level Examination Program (CLEP) covers general exams that measure achievement in five areas: English composition, social studies, natural sciences, humanities, and mathematics. You can earn a full year of college credit (30 semester hours) through the general CLEP tests. Also available through CLEP are 40 subject exams in areas such as business, history, science, and languages. For each successfully passed exam, you can earn 3 semester hours of credit.

The second testing program DANTES offers is their Subject Standardized Test (DSST). The DSSTs cover vocational and technical areas as well as the more traditional college work. You can select from 55 tests in areas as diverse as auto mechanics, forestry, and carpentry. Vocational/technical or college credits are awarded for the DSSTs, each of which has been evaluated by the American Council on Education (ACE). An ACE Guide has been developed advising colleges and universities not only on minimum scores that should be acceptable for earning college credit through the testing program, but also on credit that should be awarded for the successful completion of military schools.

One additional testing program is available. The American College Testing Proficiency Examination Program (ACT/PEP) offers 48 exams in subject areas such as nursing, management, finance, marketing, and accounting. The ACT/PEP program offers series in these areas, as well. For instance, three levels of courses can be challenged in marketing alone.

CORRESPONDENCE COURSES

Without a doubt, every soldier in the Army can further his education. Even the soldier assigned to the most remote duty site, or the one who is required to pull shift work, has the opportunity to pursue an education through correspondence courses. DANTES offers numerous independent study courses from fully accredited civilian colleges and universities. Students complete reading assignments and then exercises, submit the work for evaluation, correspond with a professor, and, in the end, take one or more examinations through the education center. Credits earned through correspondence courses equal those earned by other students in a normal classroom environment.

The major difference is the extra discipline required by the student to work diligently at the assignments without the benefit of specific deadlines and the watchful eye of a professor. Tuition assistance applies to correspondence courses under the same rules that it is applied to standard college courses.

TUITION ASSISTANCE

Most soldiers are eligible to receive 75 percent of the cost of college courses through the Army's tuition assistance program; some soldiers can receive up to 90 percent. Tuition assistance does not cover the cost of books, however.

This benefit can be considered like a scholarship, since few scholarships pay the cost-in-full for university studies. In addition, using tuition assistance does not reduce your other educational benefits (VEAP, Army College Fund, New GI Bill, or Old GI Bill). This financial assistance does not obligate you to further military service, either. It truly is free money for education. Your one obligation is to complete the course successfully. Soldiers who fail to do so are faced with additional requirements if they choose to use the aid again.

Soldiers from grades E-5 and above who have less than 14 years of service are eligible for 90 percent tuition assistance. Those with less rank, more rank, or more time in service receive 75 percent tuition assistance.

SCHOLARSHIPS, LOANS, AND GRANTS

The federal government also supports higher education through student aid programs that include grants (money that does not have to be repaid) and loans. With the current financial uncertainty due to the Gramm-Rudman balanced-budget act, it is not certain how many federal financial aid programs will continue and what form they may ultimately take. A counselor at the education center, or at the financial affairs office of the university you attend, would be in the best position to provide current information. Requesting such aid can be a time-consuming task because forms are exhaustive in detail. The effort is frequently rewarded, however, by additional money for educational purposes.

Popular pre–Gramm-Rudman federal sources included the Pell Grant and the Guaranteed Student Loan program.

Scholarships from private organizations frequently go unawarded— not because of lack of funds, but because of lack of applicants. Requirements for private scholarships can be sweeping in scope, or surprisingly narrow. For instance, one national organization provides moneys to women studying any phase of business, science, engineering, or professional studies. Another private scholarship can be awarded only to residents of New Jersey who have worked for a specified period of time as a golf caddy. Digging out information on the thousands of scholarships available can also be a time-consuming, frequently frustrating process, but again, the rewards can be most satisfying.

The best advice is to start early. Application deadlines are as varied as the qualifications themselves. The education center, university financial affairs office, and the public library are all sources of information. Also, books are published annually, listing organizations with money to give away in the form of educational scholarships. A patient, diligent search can fill any financial voids you may experience in your educational pursuit. These scholarships can also be used by your spouse or children.

LOAN REPAYMENT PROGRAM

Some soldiers may have begun their college education before enlisting in the Army. If they used a Guaranteed Student Loan (GSL), a National Defense Student Loan, or a Federally Insured Student Loan (FISL) to pay all or part of their educational costs, they may be eligible for the Army's Loan Repayment Program.

To be eligible, the soldier must have enlisted between 1 December 1980 and 30 September 1981 (FY 81) or between 1 October 1982 and 30 September 1984 (FY 83 and FY 84); in addition he must have incurred the loan between 1 October 1975 and the date of enlistment. Other eligibility requirements include enlistment in selected MOSs, an Armed Forces Qualification Test (AFQT) score of 50 or above, and no prior service. Qualifying MOSs vary according to the needs of the Army; in January 1986 more than 80 MOSs were valid. The education office can provide the current list.

Eligible soldiers should complete a DA Form 2057-5, have the local military personnel office (MILPO) verify service information on the form, and mail the form to the Department of the Army, MILPERCEN (DAPC-PLP), Alexandria, VA 22331. Then for every complete year of active duty the soldier serves, the Army will pay one-third of the outstanding loan balance at the time of enlistment, or $1,500, whichever is greater.

The Loan Repayment Program was used as an enlistment incentive and does not reduce the soldier's other educational benefits, nor does participation in the program incur additional military obligation.

VETERANS EDUCATIONAL ASSISTANCE PROGRAM (VEAP)

After the Old GI Bill was phased out for new recruits, the Army developed a participatory educational program called the Veterans Educational Assistance Program (VEAP). VEAP was soon enhanced to Super VEAP and Ultra VEAP. The Army College Fund (ACF) was then added to the VEAPs. VEAP covers soldiers who enlisted between 1 January 1977 and 30 June 1985, with interim dates established for eligibility for Super VEAP, Ultra VEAP, and ACF.

Basically, VEAP is a plan designed to help you pay for your civilian education. For each dollar you contribute to the fund, the Army contributes two. After your first term of enlistment, the funds become available to you to pay educational expenses, whether separated from the service or still on active duty attending classes on a part-time basis. You may want to consider saving the VEAP benefits until ETS or retirement and using the tuition assistance program while on active duty. In this way, you maximize all of the possible moneys that can be applied toward your education.

ACF increases the amount of government contributions. Soldiers enrolled in VEAP, scoring 50 or higher on the AFQT, and filling a "critical" MOS skill are eligible for the increased funds. Qualifying MOSs for this bonus funding program can change; an ACES official can advise on eligibility.

Under Public Law 98-525 soldiers eligible for VEAP or ACF who have not enrolled prior to 1 July 1985 can lose their benefits. If you're in this category, you should consult an ACES counselor about possible exceptions.

Soldiers who separate from service and subsequently do not use their VEAP benefits can request a refund of their contributions. Contributions made by the Army will be released to the former soldier, however, only if the individual is enrolled in post-secondary education at least part-time. Moneys are released on a monthly basis.

NEW GI BILL

Soldiers enlisting in the Army after 1 July 1985 but before 30 June 1988 are eligible for the New GI Bill, educational benefits under Chapter 30, Title 38 USC, provided they serve at least two years on active duty, have completed their high school requirements prior to the completion of the first term of enlistment, and receive an honorable discharge upon leaving the service.

Also a participatory program, the New GI Bill automatically covers all eligible recruits unless they specifically disenroll from the program. For the first 12 months of active duty, $100 is deducted from the soldier's pay. The nonrefundable deductions become the soldier's contribution to the educational fund. The soldier makes no further contributions after the first year.

Benefits under the New GI Bill are based on time in service. With two years of active duty, the maximum basic benefit is $9,000. Two years of active duty plus four years in the Selective Reserve increases the maximum to $10,800. This same figure applies to soldiers serving at least three years on active duty.

Additional benefits are also available to some soldiers through the New ACF. To be eligible, soldiers must be eligible for the New GI Bill, have completed their high school studies before entering the Army, have scored a 50 or above on the AFQT, and have enlisted in a critical MOS. (ACES counselors can advise you on the current list of critical MOSs.) The New ACF is also based on time served on active duty. Combining the basic benefits of the New GI Bill with the additional benefits of the New ACF can raise the total educational benefits to $25,200 for the soldier who spends four years on active duty in a critical MOS.

Soldiers eligible for the Old GI Bill can convert to the New GI Bill under specific circumstances. They should contact an ACES counselor for complete details. Soldiers eligible under the VEAP programs currently do not have conversion eligibility.

SCHOOLING AVAILABILITY

Almost all Army installations provide on-post educational courses at various levels: high school and college preparatory, vocational and technical, associate degree level, and baccalaureate degree level. Many posts provide master's and post-master's college course work as well. All institutions providing educational opportunities to soldiers on military installations must be accredited by the appropriate accrediting agencies. These off-campus programs are recognized in the same manner as programs taken on a college campus.

SOC and SOCAD

The Army has developed two programs to aid you in your quest to attain a college degree: Servicemembers' Opportunity Colleges (SOC) network and Servicemembers' Opportunity Colleges Associate Degree program (SOCAD).

The SOC network, developed in 1972, removes many of the obstacles soldiers faced when trying to complete degree requirements within the framework of frequent military moves. Problems of lost credit hours, varying degree requirements, and limited numbers of transfer hours were minimized through the SOC network. Member colleges recognize the special needs of the soldier by:

- Establishing liberal entrance requirements.
- Limiting residency requirements.
- Accepting nontraditional credits (generally at the levels recommended by the ACE Guide).
- Allowing more transfer hours.
- Scheduling classes at times and locations that accommodate the needs of the soldier.

At the associate degree level, the Army offers special opportunities through SOCAD. SOCAD course work applies to associate degree programs related to military specialties. Soldiers receive college credit for what they have learned through the Army, and they enhance their Army careers by improving their military skills through civilian training. SOCAD institutions agree to the same guidelines as the more general SOC program, and they offer additional benefits as well. An official evaluation is made on the soldier's nontraditional credit sources, using a standardized form accepted by all SOCAD institutions. The soldier chooses one SOCAD school as the "home institution." Once he meets the limited residency requirement at the home institution, he is free to complete the requirements at other SOCAD schools within his chosen curriculum.

Basically, SOCAD schools make getting an associate degree much easier for you. With the Army's increasing emphasis on education, this benefit can enhance your promotion potential.

Listing by Location

Before a PCS move or before requesting a particular assignment or location, it would be beneficial to the soldier pursuing a degree to know the availability of schooling at the new site. Consequently, a list has been compiled showing the institutions serving each major military installation. Most colleges listed offer courses on-post, at least on a limited basis. If the institution is close to the installation, it will sometimes elect to offer certain popular courses on site but will require students enrolling in smaller or more specialized courses to attend classes on campus.

Locations are alphabetized first by state and then by individual installations. Colleges are listed based on the programs provided and have not been alphabetized.

The degrees or certificates awarded are coded as follows:

T = Technical or vocational certificate
A = Associate degree (A.A. or A.S.)
B = Baccalaureate degree (B.A. or B.S.)
M = Master's degree (M.A. or M.S.)
P = Post-master's work (these programs may or may not culminate in a doctorate at the on-post location)

The education centers at the posts listed sometimes serve smaller installations in the nearby region. The high school and college preparatory course work has not been listed in the table, but it is available at nearly all Army installations.

Colleges

ALABAMA

Fort McClellan

	T	A	B	M
Ayers State Tech. College	T	A		
Gadsden Jr. College		A		
Jacksonville State Univ.			B	M

Fort Rucker

Alabama Aviation & Tech. College	T			
George C. Wallace Comm. College	T	A		
Embry-Riddle Aeronautical Univ.		A	B	M
Enterprise State Jr. College		A		
Troy State Univ.		A	B	M
Univ. of Southern California				M

Redstone Arsenal

J. C. Calhoun Comm. College	T	A			
J. F. Drake Tech. College	T	A			
Huntsville Voc. Center	T				
A & M Univ.		A	B	M	
Alabama Christian College		A			
Columbia College		A	B		
Univ. of Alabama		A	B	M	P
Athens College			B		
Oakwood College			B		
Florida Inst. of Technology				M	

ALASKA

Fort Greely

Central Texas College	T	A	
Univ. of Alaska		A	B

Fort Richardson

Anchorage Comm. College	T	A	
Alaska Pacific Univ.	T	A	B	M
Univ. of Alaska	T		B	M
Central Texas College		A		
Chapman College		A	B	M
LaVerne Univ.				M

Fort Wainwright

Embry-Riddle Aeronautical Univ.	T			
Tanana Valley Comm. College	T	A		
Central Texas College		A		
Univ. of Alaska		A	B	M	P

ARIZONA

Fort Huachuca

Cochise College	T	A
Pima College	T	A

Univ. of Arizona			B	M	
Univ. of Phoenix			B	M	
Golden Gate Univ.				M	

Yuma Proving Ground

Arizona Western College	T	A			
Southern Illinois Univ.			B		
Univ. of Phoenix			B	M	
Webster College				M	

CALIFORNIA

Fort Irwin

Barstow College	T	A			
Chapman College			B	M	
Univ. of Redlands			B	M	

Fort Ord

Embry-Riddle Aeronautical Univ.		A	B		
Hartnell College		A			
Monterey Peninsula College		A			
Chapman College			B	M	
Golden Gate Univ.			B	M	
Monterey Inst. of Internat'l Studies			B	M	
San Jose State Univ.			B		

Oakland Army Base

Merritt College	T	A			
Oakland Adult School Vista College	T	A			
College of Alameda		A			
Columbia College		A	B		
Lancy College		A			
California State			B		
Golden Gate Univ.			B	M	P
San Francisco State Univ.			B		
Univ. of California—Berkley			B		
Univ. of San Francisco			B		

Presidio of San Francisco

City College of San Francisco	T	A			
Comm. College Ctrs. of San Francisco	T				
San Francisco State Univ.	T		B	M	P
Indian Valley Comm. College		A			
Golden Gate Univ.			B	M	P

	T	A	B	M	P
San Francisco Conservatory of Music			B	M	
Univ. of California—Berkley			B	M	P
Univ. of San Francisco			B	M	P
Univ. of California—San Francisco				M	P

Sacramento Army Depot

	T	A	B	M	P
American River College	T	A			
Consumnes River College	T	A			
Sacramento City College	T	A			
Sierra College		A			
Chapman College			B	M	
Golden Gate Univ.			B	M	
Pacific Christian College			B		
Sacramento State Univ.			B		
Univ. of California—Davis			B	M	P
California State Univ.				M	
Univ. of Southern California				M	P
McGeorge School of Law					P

Sharpe Army Depot

	T	A	B	M	P
Delta College	T				
Woodruff Voc. Center	T				
San Joaquin Delta College		A			
California State College			B		
Chapman College			B	M	
Pacific Christian College			B		
Univ. of the Pacific			B	M	P

Sierra Army Depot

	T	A	B	M	P
Lassen College	T	A			
California State College			B	M	
Univ. of Chicago			B	M	

COLORADO

Fitzsimons Army Medical Center

	T	A	B	M	P
Arapahoe Comm. College	T				
Park College		A	B		
Regis College		A	B		
Univ. of Colorado			B	M	
Univ. of Northern Colorado			B	M	
Webster College				M	
Univ. of Denver					P

Fort Carson

	T	A	B	M	P
Chapman College	T		B	M	
Pikes Peak Comm. College	T	A			
Regis College		A	B		
Southern Illinois Univ.			B		
Univ. of Colorado at Col. Springs			B		
Univ. of Northern Colorado				M	
Univ. of Southern California				M	
Webster College				M	
Univ. of Denver					P

DISTRICT OF COLUMBIA

Harkins Building Army Education Ctr.

	T	A	B	M	P
Univ. of the District of Columbia		A	B		
Catholic Univ.				M	
George Washington Univ.				M	

The Pentagon

	T	A	B	M	P
Northern Virginia Comm. College		A			
Univ. of Maryland		A	B		P
American Univ.				M	P
Catholic Univ. of America				M	P
Georgetown Univ.				M	P
George Washington Univ.				M	P
Univ. of Oklahoma				M	
Univ. of Southern California				M	
(Plus many other institutions)					

Walter Reed Army Medical Center

	T	A	B	M	P
Essex Comm. College		A			
Montgomery College		A			
Southern Illinois Univ.			B		
Univ. of Maryland			B		
Central Michigan Univ.				M	
George Washington Univ.					P

GEORGIA

Fort Benning

	T	A	B	M	P
Columbus Area Voc. Tech. School	T				
Columbus College	T	A	B	M	P
Chattahoochee Valley Comm. College	T	A			
Embry-Riddle Aeronautical Univ.		A	B		

	T	A	B	M	P
Troy State Univ.		A	B	M	
Georgia State Univ.				M	P

Fort Gordon

	T	A	B	M	P
Aiken Tech. Inst.	T				
Georgia Military College		A			
Medical College of Georgia		A	B	M	P
Augusta College			B	M	
Paine College			B		
Southern Illinois Univ.			B		
Georgia Inst. of Technology				M	
Georgia Southern College				M	

Fort McPherson

	T	A	B	M	P
Atlanta Area Technical	T				
Clayton Jr. College	T	A			
DeKalb Comm. College	T	A			
Marietta-Cobb Area Voc. Tech.	T				
Atlanta Jr. College		A			
Clark College			B		
Morris Brown College			B		
Georgia State College			B	M	P
Georgia Inst. of Technology			B	M	P
Kennesaw College			B		
Mercer Univ.—Atlanta			B	M	
Morehouse College			B		
Northern Georgia College			B		
St. Leo College			B		
Agnes Scott College			B		
Oglethorpe Univ.			B		
Spellman College			B		
Atlanta Univ.				M	P
Central Michigan Univ.				M	
Emory Univ.				M	

Fort Stewart/Hunter Army Airfield

	T	A	B	M	P
Savannah Area Voc. Tech. School	T				
Armstrong State College		A	B	M	
Brunswick Jr. College		A			
Georgia Southern College		A	B	M	P
St. Leo College		A	B		
Savannah State College		A	B		
Central Michigan Univ.				M	

HAWAII

Fort Shafter

Hawaii Pacific College	T	A	B	
Honolulu Comm. College	T	A		
Kapiolani Comm. College	T	A		
Leeward Comm. College	T	A		
Univ. of Hawaii	T	A	B	M P
Windward Comm. College	T	A		
Chaminade Univ.		A	B	M
Embry-Riddle Aeronautical Univ.		A	B	M
Brigham Young Univ.		A	B	
Antioch Univ.			B	M
Hawaii Loa College			B	
Roosevelt Univ.			B	
Wayland Baptist Univ.			B	
West Oahu College			B	
Central Michigan Univ.				M
Univ. of Oklahoma				M
Univ. of Southern California				M P

Schofield Barracks

Hawaii Pacific College	T	A	B	
Honolulu Comm. College	T	A		
Kapiolani Comm. College	T	A		
Leeward Comm. College	T	A		
Roosevelt Univ.	T		B	
Univ. of Hawaii	T	A	B	M P
Windward Comm. College	T	A		
Chaminade Univ.		A	B	M
Embry-Riddle Aeronautical Univ.		A	B	M
Brigham Young Univ.		A	B	
Antioch Univ.			B	M
Wayland Baptist Univ.			B	
West Oahu College			B	
Central Michigan Univ.				M
Univ. of Oklahoma				M
Univ. of Southern California				M P

Tripler Army Medical Center

Hawaii Pacific College	T	A	B
Honolulu Comm. College	T	A	
Kapiolani Comm. College	T	A	
Leeward Comm. College	T	A	

	T	A	B	M	P
Univ. of Hawaii	T	A	B	M	P
Windward Comm. College	T	A			
Chaminade Univ.		A	B	M	
Embry-Riddle Aeronautical Univ.		A	B	M	
Brigham Young Univ.		A	B		
Antioch Univ.			B	M	
Hawaii Loa College			B		
Roosevelt Univ.			B		
West Oahu College			B		
Wayland Baptist Univ.			B		
Central Michigan Univ.				M	
Univ. of Oklahoma				M	
Univ. of Southern California				M	P

ILLINOIS

Fort Sheridan

	T	A	B	M	P
Chicago City Wide College	T	A			
College of Lake County	T	A			
Columbia College		A	B		
DePaul Univ.			B	M	P
Governors State Univ.			B		
Loyola Univ.			B	M	P
Northeastern Illinois Univ.			B	M	P
Univ. of Illinois			B	M	P
Western Illinois Univ.			B		
Lake Forest College				M	
Webster College				M	
Northwestern Univ.					P
Univ. of Chicago					P

St. Louis Area Support Center

	T	A	B	M	P
Belleville Area College	T	A			
Maryville College	T	A	B		
St. Louis Comm. College	T	A	B	M	P
Columbia College		A	B		
Harris Stowe College			B		
Park College			B		
Tarkio College			B		
Univ. of Missouri			B	M	P
Washington Univ.			B	M	P
Webster College			B	M	
Southern Illinois Univ.				M	P

INDIANA

Fort Benjamin Harrison

Indiana Voc. Tech. College	T			
Vincennes Univ.		A		
Ball State Univ.			B M P
Butler Univ.			B M P
Indiana Univ./Purdue Univ. at Indianapolis			B M P
Indiana Central Univ.			B M
Indiana State Univ.			B M
Indiana Univ. at Bloomington			B M
Marian College			B
Purdue Univ.			B M

KANSAS

Fort Leavenworth

Leavenworth High School	T			
Kansas City—Kansas Comm. College		A		
Park College		A	B	
St. Mary College		A	B	
Wichita State		A	B M	
Univ. of Kansas			B M P	
Univ. of Southern California			M	
Univ. of Missouri				P

Fort Riley

Central Texas College	T	A		
Kansas Tech. Inst.	T	A	B	
Kansas State Univ.		A	B M P	
Kansas Wesleyan Univ.		A	B	
Wichita State		A	B M	
Univ. of Southern California			M	

KENTUCKY

Fort Campbell

Austin Peay State Univ.	T	A B M P	
Central Texas College	T		
Murray State Univ.	T	M	
Embry-Riddle Aeronautical Univ.		A B M	
Univ. of Southern California		M	
Tennessee State Univ.			P

Fort Knox

Eastern Kentucky Univ.		A	B	
Elizabethtown Comm. College		A		
Embry-Riddle Aeronautical Univ.		A	B	M
Univ. of Louisville		A	B	M	P
Western Kentucky Univ.		A	B	M
Univ. of Kentucky			B	M	P
Univ. of Southern California				M

LOUISIANA

Fort Polk

TAD Tech. Services Corp.	T		
Northwestern State Univ. of La.		A	
Northwestern State Univ.			B	M

MARYLAND

Aberdeen Proving Ground

Cecil Comm. College	T	A		
Comm. College of Baltimore	T	A		
Dundalk Comm. College	T	A		
Essex Comm. College	T	A		
Hartford Comm. College	T	A		
Univ. of Maryland		A	B	M	P
Coppin State College			B	M
Johns Hopkins Univ.			B	M	P
Loyola College			B	M
Morgan State Univ.			B	M
Towson State Univ.			B	M
Univ. of Baltimore			B	M	P
Univ. of Delaware			B	M	P
Central Michigan Univ.				M
Florida Inst. of Technology				M

Fort Detrick

Frederick Comm. College	T		
Hood College			B	M
Mount Saint Mary's College			B
Univ. of Maryland			B
Frostburg State College				M

Fort Meade

	T	A	B	M	P
Anne Arundel Comm. College	T	A			
Catonsville Comm. College		A			
Charles County Comm. College		A			
Essex Comm. College		A			
Howard Comm. College		A			
Montgomery College		A			
Coppin State College			B		
Loyola College			B		
Morgan State Univ.			B		
Towson State Univ.			B		
Univ. of Baltimore			B	M	
Univ. of Maryland			B	M	P
American Univ.				M	
Catholic Univ.				M	P
Central Michigan Univ.				M	
Georgetown Univ.				M	
Johns Hopkins Univ.				M	P
George Washington Univ.				M	P
Regents, Univ. of the State of N.Y.		A	B		

Fort Ritchie

	T	A	B	M	P
Hagerstown Jr. College	T	A			
Pennsylvania State Univ.		A			
Univ. of Maryland		A	B		
Capitol Inst. of Technology			B		
Gettysburg College			B		
Johns Hopkins Univ.			B		
Mount Saint Mary's College			B	M	
Shepard College			B		
Shippensburg State Univ.			B	M	
Univ. of Baltimore			B		
Frostburg State College				M	

MASSACHUSETTS

Fort Devens

	T	A	B	M	P
Anna Maria College	T				P
Assumption College	T				
Fisher Jr. College	T	A			
Fitchburg State College	T		B	M	
Middlesex Comm. College	T	A			
New Hampshire Comm. College	T				

	T	A	B	M	P
Quinsigamond Comm. College	T	A			
Wentworth Inst.	T	A	B		
Boston Univ.		A	B	M	P
Central New England College		A	B		
Mount Wachusett Comm. College		A			
Northeastern Univ.		A	B	M	P
Northern Essex Comm. College		A			
Univ. of Lowell		A	B		
Framingham State College			B		
Suffolk Univ.			B		
New England Conservatory of Music			B	M	
Western New England College			B	M	
Worcester State College			B	M	
Clark Univ.				M	P
Worcester Polytechnical Inst.				M	
Boston College					P
Harvard Univ.					P

MICHIGAN

Selfridge ANG Base

	T	A	B	M	P
Macomb County Comm. College	T	A			
Northwood Inst.		A	B		
Oakland Univ.			B	M	P
Univ. of Detroit			B	M	P
Walsh College of Accounting & Bus.			B	M	
Wayne State Univ.			B	M	P
Central Michigan Univ.				M	
Florida Inst. of Technology				M	
Western Michigan Univ.					P

MISSOURI

Fort Leonard Wood

	T	A	B	M	P
Central Texas College	T	A			
Columbia College		A	B		
Drury College		A	B	M	
Univ. of Missouri				M	P
Webster College				M	

NEW JERSEY

Fort Dix

	T	A
Burlington County College	T	A

Burlington County Voc. Tech. Schl.	T			
Brookdale Comm. College	T			
Ocean County College	T			
Thomas Edison Comm. College		A	B	
Regents, Univ. of the State of N.Y.		A	B	
Southern Illinois Univ.			B	M
Trenton State College			B	
Central Michigan Univ.				M
Monmouth College				M
Rider College				M

Fort Monmouth

Brookdale Comm. College	T	A			
Monmouth College	T	A	B		
County College of Morris		A			
Fairleigh Dickinson Univ.			B	M	
Kean College			B		
Florida Inst. of Technology				M	
Rutgers Univ.					P

NEW MEXICO

White Sands Missile Range

Florida Inst. of Technology				M	
New Mexico State Univ.	T	A	B	M	P

NEW YORK

Fort Drum

Jefferson Comm. College	A

Fort Hamilton

Ocean County College	T			
City Univ. of New York Tech. Inst.		A	B	
John Jay College of Criminal Justice		A	B	M
York College of the City of N.Y.		A		
Long Island Univ.			B	M
New York Univ.			B	M
Saint John's Univ.			B	
Brooklyn College				M
Central Michigan Univ.				M
City Univ. of New York				M
Russell Sage College				M

Seneca Army Depot

	T	A	B	M	P
Comm. College of the Finger Lakes	T	A			
Cayuga County Comm. College		A			
Regents, Univ. of the State of N.Y.		A	B		
Elmira College			B	M	
Ithaca College			B	M	
Rochester Inst. of Technology			B	M	
Syracuse Univ.				M	P
Univ. of Rochester					P

United States Military Academy

	T	A	B	M	
Orange County Comm. College	T	A			
State Univ. of New York	T		B		
John Jay College of Criminal Justice		A	B	M	
Rockland Comm. College		A			
Saint Thomas Aquinas		A	B		
Mount Saint Mary's College			B		
C. W. Post, Long Island Univ.				M	

NORTH CAROLINA

Fort Bragg

	T	A	B	M	P
Fayetteville Tech. Inst.	T	A			
Campbell Univ.	T		B	M	
Embry-Riddle Aeronautical Univ.		A	B	M	
Fayetteville State Univ.		A	B		
Golden Gate Univ.		A	B	M	
Methodist College		A	B		
Shaw Univ.			B		
Southern Illinois Univ.			B		
North Carolina State Univ.				M	
Webster College				M	
Nova Univ.					P

OKLAHOMA

Ft. Sill

	T	A	B
Caddo-Kiowa Vo-Tech	T		
Cameron Univ.	T	A	B
Canadian Valley Vo-Tech	T		
Central Texas College	T		
Great Plains Area	T		
Lawton High School	T		
Red River Vo-Tech	T		

Western Oklahoma State College	T	A		
Midwestern Univ.		A	B	M
Oklahoma Univ.		A	B	M	P
Southwestern Univ.		A	B	M
Univ. of Science and Arts		A	B
Webster College		A	B	M

PENNSYLVANIA

Carlisle Barracks

Harrisburg Area Comm. College	T	A		
Univ. Center		A	B	M
Shippensburg State Univ.			B	M
Penn State				M

SOUTH CAROLINA

Fort Jackson

Midlands Tech. College	T	A		
Park College		A	B
Univ. of South Carolina		A	B	M	P
Coker College			B

TEXAS

Fort Bliss

El Paso Public Schools	T			
El Paso Comm. College	T	A		
Park College		A	B
Univ. of Texas at El Paso			B	M
Webster College				M

Fort Hood

Central Texas College		A		
American Technical Univ.			B	M
Univ. of Mary Hardin Baylor			B

Fort Sam Houston

Our Lady of the Lake Univ.	T		B	M
Saint Philip's College	T	A		
Univ. of Texas Health Service Ctr.	T			M	P
Saint Mary's Univ.		A	B	M	P
San Antonio College		A		
Southwest Texas State Univ.		A	B	M

	T	A	B	M	P
Texas Lutheran College		A			
Incarnate Word College			B	M	
Park College			B		
Trinity Univ.			B	M	
Texas A & M				M	P
Univ. of Texas at San Antonio				M	
Webster College				M	

UTAH

Dugway Proving Ground

	T	A	B	M	P
Utah Tech. College	T	A			
Weber State College		A	B		
Columbia College		A	B		
Brigham Young Univ.		A	B	M	P
Univ. of Utah			B	M	P
Utah State Univ.			B	M	
Westminster College			B	M	

VIRGINIA

Arlington Hall Station

	T	A	B	M	P
Arlington County Adult Learning Ctr.	T				
Paragon Associates	T				
Reading Techniques	T				
Univ. of Virginia	T				
Regents, Univ. of the State of N.Y.		A			
Northern Virginia Comm. College		A			
Park College		A	B		
Strayer College		A	B		
Univ. of Maryland			B	M	
American Univ.				M	

Fort Belvoir

	T	A	B	M	P
Fairfax Skill Center	T				
Univ. of Maryland	T	A	B		P
Univ. of Virginia	T			M	
Montgomery Comm. College		A			
Northern Virginia Comm. College		A			
Univ. of the District of Columbia		A			
American Univ.			B	M	P
Catholic Univ.			B	M	P
Howard Univ.			B	M	P

	T	A	B	M	P
George Washington Univ.			B	M	P
George Mason Univ.				M	P
Virginia Polytechnic Inst.				M	

Fort Eustis

	T	A	B	M	P
Virginia Peninsula Voc.-Tech. Ctr.	T				
Virginia Beach Voc.-Tech. Ctr.	T				
Embry-Riddle Aeronautical Univ.		A	B		
Thomas Nelson Comm. College		A			
Saint Leo College		A	B		
Tidewater Comm. College		A			
Christopher Newport College			B		
College of William and Mary			B	M	P
Hampton Univ.			B	M	
Norfolk State Univ.			B	M	
Old Dominion Univ.			B		P
Golden Gate Univ.				M	
George Washington Univ.				M	

Fort Lee

	T	A	B	M	P
John Tyler Comm. College	T	A			
Central Texas College		A			
Saint Leo College		A	B		
Virginia State Univ.			B	M	
Chapman College				M	
Florida Inst. of Technology				M	

Fort Monroe

	T	A	B	M	P
Peninsula Voc.-Tech. Center	T				
Embry-Riddle Aeronautical Univ.		A	B	M	
Thomas Nelson Comm. College		A			
Tidewater Comm. College		A			
Saint Leo College		A	B		
College of William & Mary			B	M	P
Hampton Univ.			B		
Christopher Newport College			B		
Norfolk State Univ.			B		
Old Dominion Univ.			B	M	P
Virginia Wesleyan			B		
Florida Inst. of Technology				M	
Golden Gate Univ.				M	
Univ. of Southern California				M	
George Washington Univ.				M	P

Fort Myer

	T	A	B	M	P
Arlington County Adult Education	T				
Northern Virginia Comm. College	T	A			
Anne Arundel Comm. College		A			
Park College		A	B		
Prince George's Comm. College		A			
Strayer College		A	B		
Univ. of the District of Columbia		A	B		
Univ. of Maryland		A	B		
American Univ.			B		
Bowie State College			B		
Catholic Univ.			B	M	
Gallaudet College			B		
George Mason Univ.			B		
Georgetown Univ.			B	M	
Howard Univ.			B		
Johns Hopkins Univ.			B		
Marymount College of Virginia			B	M	
Univ. of Baltimore			B		
George Washington Univ.			B	M	
Central Michigan Univ.				M	
Golden Gate Univ.				M	

Hoffman Building

	T	A	B	M	P
Northern Virginia Comm. College	T	A			
Univ. of Virginia	T				
Park College		A	B		
Univ. of Maryland			B		
Catholic Univ. of America				M	
Central Michigan Univ.				M	
Univ. of Southern California				M	
Florida Inst. of Technology					P
George Mason Univ.					P

Vint Hill Farms Station

	T	A	B	M	P
Fauquier County Voc. Adult Education	T				
Northern Virginia Comm. College	T	A			
Regents, Univ. of the State of N.Y.		A	B		
Univ. of Virginia		A	B		
George Mason Univ.			B	M	P
Central Michigan Univ.				M	
Virginia Polytechnic Univ.					P

WASHINGTON

Fort Lewis

Clover Park Voc.-Tech. Inst.	T		
L. H. Bates Voc.-Tech. Inst.	T		
Central Texas College	A		
Fort Steilaccom Comm. College	A		
Saint Martin's College	A	B	
Embry-Riddle Aeronautical Univ.		B	
Pacific Lutheran Univ.			M
Univ. of Puget Sound			M
Univ. of Southern California			M

Schooling Overseas

Overseas assignments are serviced by contract institutions. In Europe, for instance, five colleges provide vocational, technical, associate, and baccalaureate programs for all Army installations. Five provide graduate programs as well, although there is overlap among the groups. Overseas assignments are listed only by regions, and then the colleges that serve the entire region are listed.

Europe

The Army has 32 education centers in Europe that service the military community. The educational program is a comprehensive package, with services provided to soldiers in even the most remote of the 400 casernes and garrisons. Three colleges provide technical certificate education programs throughout the region: Big Bend Community College, Central Texas College, and City Colleges of Chicago. Each of the three also offers studies at the baccalaureate degree level. Two other universities provide study at this level as well — Embry-Riddle Aeronautical University and the University of Maryland.

Technical programs include offerings for certificates in air conditioning, applied and mid-management, automotive technology, communications, data processing, drafting, electronics, engineering technician, emergency medical technician, food services, law enforcement, and small engine repair.

The undergraduate programs include art, aviation maintenance, broadcast electronics, business management, computer science, health facilities management, hotel/motel management, paralegal studies, photography, real estate, recreation, secretarial science, and transportation.

Graduate programs are also plentiful. Embry-Riddle Aeronautical University, Ball State University, Boston University, the University of Oklahoma, and the University of Southern California offer degree programs at the master's level. Boston University expands its curriculum to post-master's work, as well.

The soldier's choices for the graduate (master's and post-master's) level are somewhat more limited. They include aeronautical studies, business administration, computer information systems, counseling, education, engineering, human relations, international relations, nursing, public administration, and systems management.

As is true with stateside assignments, the soldier has a wealth of educational opportunities at the high school level, the Basic Skills Education Program (BSEP) level, and the Career Soldier's Education Program (CSEP) level.

Japan/Okinawa

Educational opportunities in Japan and Okinawa are more limited than those in Europe. A soldier can still complete his secondary education by GED, however, and can participate in college preparatory programs. Language programs include German and Japanese.

Only one undergraduate school, the University of Maryland, services this region. It offers associate degrees with majors in general curriculum and Japanese studies. In addition, students can work toward baccalaureate degrees in Asian studies, business and management, government and politics, history, psychology, and sociology.

At the master's degree level, the University of Oklahoma offers the opportunity for soldiers to study public administration. In addition, the University of Southern California allows students to study two areas at the graduate level: education and systems management. Post-master's programs are not available.

Panama

Soldiers stationed in Panama can take advantage of a full range of course work at the secondary and college preparatory levels, including BSEP and ESL. Vocational/technical training is also available in automobile mechanics, electricity, electronics, television repair, and welding. Spanish is available in the language program.

Four universities offer a wide range of college level programs in this area. Florida State University offers certificates with major fields of study in corrections and law enforcement. In addition, they offer an associate degree in general studies and baccalaureate degrees in business, English, inter-American studies, international affairs, social studies, and Spanish.

The Panama Canal College offers certificate programs in accounting, data processing, and secretarial studies. Their associate degrees are the highest degrees awarded by the college. The fourteen majors offered are accounting, art, behavioral science, biological science, business administration, criminal justice, English, foreign language, history, learning resource technology, mathematical science, physical education, radiological technology, and secretarial administration.

Nova University provides baccalaureate and master's degree programs. At the undergraduate level, students can study technological management. At the graduate level, students may choose among business administration, human resource management, and public administration.

The last school serving the soldiers stationed in Panama is the University of Oklahoma, offering master's degrees in five areas: business administration, educational psychology, human relations, management, and public administration.

Puerto Rico

The on-post educational opportunities in Puerto Rico are quite limited. A full curricular range is available, however, from the associate level to the post-master's level for students willing to travel to the off-post campuses located from three to fifty miles from Fort Buchanan.

Only two skill development programs offer certificates on post. These include Los Angeles Community College's certificate in emergency medical technician, and the Manpower Business Training Institute's certificate in business skills. Secondary and college preparatory programs on post include GED completion, BSEP, and ESL. Language training is available in Spanish and German.

Off-post universities and their distances from the post include:

- Bayamon Central University (10 miles).
- Catholic University (50 miles).
- Inter-American University (3 miles).
- Sacred Heart University (5 miles).
- University of Puerto Rico (10 miles).
- World University (10 miles).

South Korea

Soldiers stationed in South Korea can take advantage of a full range of educational opportunities without leaving the post, whether they are assigned in the northern region (Camp Red Cloud or Camp Greaves); in the southern region (Camp Pusan); or any of the 12 other camps in between.

The secondary level course work includes GED, high school diploma, college preparatory courses, languages (German, Japanese, and Korean), BSEP, and ESL.

Central Texas College offers certificates and associate degrees in automobile mechanics, food services, and welding. The only other associate degree program is offered by the University of Maryland, in business management and general studies. The University of Maryland also provides opportunities at the baccalaureate level, with degree programs in Asian studies, general management, government and politics, and history. No other colleges offer baccalaureate programs in Korea.

At the graduate level, two schools are available—the University of Oklahoma and the University of Southern California. Between the two, students may study human relations, public administration, systems management, and education. Post-master's programs are not available.

4

Excelling

Every day, somewhere in the Army, soldiers are being recognized for their outstanding performance. Although these soldiers are from different units and hold different MOSs, they all have one characteristic in common— motivation. It takes a motivated soldier to be skilled and knowledgeable in his assigned duties as well as in a variety of military subjects. Such motivation will assist the soldier in gaining recognition, whether through a promotion board; a Soldier of the Month/Quarter/Year board; or an outstanding evaluation report.

MEETING THE BOARD

In order to be declared the best in an extremely competitive situation, when most of the other candidates are also motivated to win, it is essential for you to know exactly what is expected of you before meeting a board. Also, knowing how the system works will remove the edge of nervousness created by "unknown factors."

Although board guidelines vary slightly from post to post, philosophically, most Soldier of the Month boards are created to identify and recognize individual soldiers who have exemplary conduct, efficiency, appearance, and overall military performance. Other norms apply as well. Generally, soldiers in grades E4 and below (excluding corporals) will compete for Soldier of the Month. Soldiers in grades E5 and E6 and corporals will compete for NCO of the Month. Often, however, E4 promotables will compete on the NCO boards.

Boards are normally composed of three or more voting members. Soldier and/or NCO of the Month boards will frequently have the First Sergeant of Headquarters Company for a given post assigned as board president. Both candidates and board members should be in Class A uniforms, with all decorations and ribbons. (See *Promotions* in this chapter for more details on board makeup; and chapter 6 for answers to any specific questions on wearing of the uniform, decorations, and ribbons.)

Reporting to the Board

On the day of the board, most candidates are extremely nervous. Relaxing as much as possible is the first step toward success.

Candidates should knock on the door of the board room and enter when directed. When approaching the president of the board, the soldier should use distinct, crisp movements. Generally, the president of the board will be flanked on both sides by other board members. The soldier should come to attention in front of the president, render a hand salute (holding it until returned by the president), and report. The next move should be directed by the president.

Responding to the Board

All board members will evaluate the candidate on his military bearing, uniform and appearance, oral presentation, and knowledge of general topics, such as chain of command, current events, and Army programs. In addition, each board member will ask the candidate several specific questions covering a wide range of military subjects. Only the member asking the specific question will evaluate the candidate's response. A typical list of military subjects is included later in this section.

The candidate should take special care to review the Soldier's Manual of Common Tasks (STP 21-1-SMCT) for the appropriate skill level. In addition, the job description of the next higher grade for the soldier's MOS (as provided in AR 611-201) is an excellent source of study before meeting the board.

Current events topics can include any local, state, national, or international event that has been reported frequently in the newspapers, broadcast media, or news magazines. Good sources for keeping abreast of current events are: *USA Today,* a national newspaper providing excellent coverage of national and international news; *Army Times,* for military news; the local newspaper, for community affairs; and the post newspaper and unit bulletin board, for those matters even closer to home. The soldier can supplement his reading by listening to both local and national news broadcasts. Trying to catch up on current events a few days before the board meets, however, will only cause confusion and increased nervousness.

Army programs cover a wide range of possibilities, from the drug and alcohol abuse program to education programs; from the equal opportunity program to the weight control program; and from the Army Community Service to the Army Emergency Relief program. This list is far from comprehensive.

Knowledge of the chain of command should be complete and up-to-date (see chain of command lists later in this section). If in doubt, the soldier should contact the appropriate office on post and request the name of the current commander or NCO.

Candidates should prefix responses to board members with the proper rank of the individual (i.e., "Sergeant Major," "First Sergeant," or "Sergeant," as appropriate). Responses should be accurate, honest, and concise. An incorrect answer is more damaging than a straightforward comment such as "Sergeant, I do not know the answer." If the soldier does not understand the question being asked, he should ask the board member to repeat or rephrase the question.

The soldier should direct his responses to the individual asking the question. Eye contact is important and should be maintained.

The most impressive responses often include a rephrasing of the question by the candidate; for instance, "Sergeant, the two parts of a drill command are. . . ." Responses can be greatly weakened by mumbling, muttering, displaying nervous mannerisms, overusing hand gestures, pointing a finger at a board member to emphasize a point, or speaking too softly. The soldier can compensate for a quivering voice by speaking a bit more loudly.

Dismissal by the Board

Once the president has indicated that the board has concluded its questioning, the candidate should come to attention in front of the president, render a hand salute, hold the salute until it is returned by the president, and then exit the room and close the door. Crisp movements during the exit create a final positive image.

After exiting the room, the soldier should not discuss questions with other candidates. Doing so only gives an advantage to the competitors.

Other Important Tips

An impeccably dressed soldier makes a positive first impression, which can be persuasive. Great care should be taken with the uniform. Often a soldier will have a set of Class A uniforms set aside for special occasions, such as boards or parades. The uniform should be carried to the board site where the soldier should dress 30 minutes before the scheduled appearance before the board. After dressing, the servicemember should not sit down.

New awards and decorations, as well as new insignia, should be purchased if the soldier's current set is either soiled or scratched. Care should be taken in the alignment and position of uniform items.

Pulling loose threads from a uniform can often complicate the original problem. Loose threads should be cut off. Also, a few paper clips dropped in the uniform pocket can avert an embarrassing moment if one of the button backings breaks right before the soldier is to report to the board. Another emergency measure is carrying a few small erasers to replace insignia or ribbon backings if they should be lost.

Chain of Command

Commander in Chief	(President of the United States)
Secretary of Defense	_____
Secretary of the Army	_____
Chairman, JCS	_____
Chief of Staff, Army	_____
MACOM Commander	_____
Post Commander	_____
Brigade Commander	_____
Battalion Commander	_____
Company Commander	_____
Platoon Leader	_____

Enlisted Chain of Command

Sergeant Major of the Army	_____
MACOM Command Sergeant Major	_____
Post Command Sergeant Major	_____
Brigade Command Sergeant Major	_____
Battalion Command Sergeant Major	_____

First Sergeant _____
Platoon Sergeant _____
Squad Leader _____

Possible Military Subject Areas

Adverse Environment and Terrain	Map Reading
CBR/NBC (Mopp)	Military Customs/Courtesies
Code of Conduct	Military Intelligence
Drills & Ceremonies	Military Justice (USMJ)
Field Sanitation	Military Tactics
First Aid	Military Unit History
Flags	M16 Rifle
Geneva Convention	Night Operations
Guard Duty	Supply (economy)
Inclement Weather Operations	Survival
Leadership	

PROMOTIONS

"Moving up through the ranks" is important to every soldier. Promotions mean more than an increase in pay. They represent recognition for a job well done, a vote of confidence in future potential, and an increase in responsibility and leadership opportunities. The Army uses promotions not only to fill spaces with qualified soldiers but also to provide career progression for the individual and to recognize those soldiers best qualified to fill higher positions of authority.

The primary qualification for promotion is the mastering of skills needed to perform the duties in the new grade. Technical expertise in the soldier's field of specialization is a consideration in the promotion process, but personal traits, professionalism as a soldier, and leadership are not overlooked. Before soldiers can expect to be promoted, they must be outstanding in their present grade and level of responsibility.

A soldier may meet all of the minimum time-related requirements for promotion, but may not be ready to assume the higher grade. If the soldier is not recommended for promotion by the commander once he has met minimum eligibility (without waivers), the supervisor is required to counsel the soldier on those areas that are deficient. With weaknesses thus identified, the soldier can begin the process of improvement, setting goals in self-improvement and training, which can lead to a more satisfying military career.

Promotion to E2

The only promotion in the Army that can be said to be automatic is the promotion to E2. Once the soldier has been on active duty in the Army for 6 months, he is promoted, unless such promotion is blocked for a serious cause by the unit commander (see the section on nonpromotable status). Local commanders can, however, promote a deserving soldier faster. Accelerated promotions can be given to a soldier with 4 months of time in service. The number of these promotions is limited. Not more than 20 percent of the soldiers in grade E2, assigned or attached to a given unit, may have less than 6 months' active duty time.

Training advancements are another manner in which a soldier may be accelerated more quickly than normal. Basic Combat Training (BCT) and One Station Unit Training (OSUT) company commanders may award accelerated training promotions to up to 3 percent of the graduates, with no restrictions on time in service.

NBC Exercise

Promotion to E3

After the initial promotion to E2, no other promotions are automatic or mandatory. Unit commanders still have the authority to promote soldiers to the private first class rank, and accelerated schedules are still possible.

Under normal promotion consideration, the soldier must have 12 months of time in service and 4 months of time in grade E2 to be considered for E3. The 4 months of time in grade can be reduced to 2 months if the time in service requirements are met. No restrictions exist on the time in grade reductions.

Accelerated promotions are possible at the discretion of the unit commander when an outstanding soldier has at least 6 months in service and 2 months in grade. Again, only 20 percent of the soldiers assigned or attached to a given unit may be in grade E3 with less than 12 months of service.

Promotion to E4

Much like the previous two promotions, advancement to E4 is usually awarded by the unit commander. Normal and accelerated promotions are still possible. The most significant difference between this promotion and earlier promotions is that the soldier *may* be required to meet a local selection board and to have taken the Skill Qualification Test (SQT).

Without any waivers, a soldier can be promoted to E4 after 24 months in service and 6 months in grade (at E3). Half of the time in grade requirements can be waived without restrictions.

Outstanding performance can again be recognized through accelerated promotions, with a minimum time in service requirement of 12 months and a minimum time in grade requirement of 3 months. Only 20 percent of the soldiers attached or assigned to a given unit may hold the E4 rank with less than 24 months of service.

When time in service waivers are to be considered, local commanders can choose to convene a selection board to identify those soldiers most qualified to receive the accelerated promotions. Boards are governed by specific rules. They must have a president (who may or may not be able to vote), a recorder (who is never allowed to vote), and at least three voting members. Majority vote will determine which soldiers are to be promoted. All members must be in grades higher than E4, at least one voting member must be of the same sex as the soldier before the board, and the board must contain minority ethnic groups.

Soldiers appearing before the board who are not selected for promotion must be counseled on which areas need improvement. A Report of Board Proceedings and a recommended promotion list must be prepared and maintained in the unit files.

Promotions to E5 and E6

Above grade E4, promotions become more complicated and are based on an Army-wide point system. Here, Headquarters, Department of the Army (HQDA) is involved. HQDA considers the needs of the Army by grade and by MOS. Using the projected needs formula, HQDA then establishes point cutoff scores for both primary and secondary zones. Zones can be compared to normal promotions and accelerated promotion at the lower grades. Through the point system, the best soldiers Army-wide can be promoted, versus the best soldiers in a given unit. Only field grade commanders (O6 and above) are authorized to award E5 and E6 promotions. This requirement also ensures that promotions are removed from the unit level.

Similar to earlier promotions, time in service and time in grade requirements are established. Appearance before a selection board is required. Waivers are permitted on some requirements, but no more than two waivers may be granted to an individual. Waivers, which permit promotion from the secondary zone, are reserved for the truly exceptional soldier and must be approved personally by the promotion authority. Secondary zone promotions are intended to serve as an incentive, a goal for soldiers "who strive for excellence and whose accomplishments, demonstrated capacity for leadership, and marked potential warrant promotion ahead of their peers" (AR 600-200).

For promotion to E5, the soldier must have served 8 months as an E4, although half of the time in grade requirements can be waived. For primary zone consideration, the soldier must have 36 months in service; for secondary zone consideration the time in service requirement is reduced to 24 months, although the reduction in time in service requirement is counted as one of the two allowable waivers. In addition, the soldier must be in a promotable status, have the recommendation of his unit commander, and appear before the board. None of these requirements can be waived. Soldiers can appear before the E5 promotion selection board up to 3 months before they are eligible to be promoted (33 months in service for primary zone; 21 months in service for secondary zone).

Many of the same types of requirements are imposed on soldiers considered for promotion to E6. Time in grade at E5 is 10 months, although half may be waived. Time in service requirements are 84 months (7 years) for the primary zone and 60 months (5 years) for the secondary zone. Promotion from the secondary zone constitutes one of the two waivers for time in service. Three months before time in service requirements are met, soldiers are allowed to meet the board. The conditions of promotable status, commander's recommendations, and board appearance are still required and cannot be waived.

The SQT and Its Impact on Promotions

The Skill Qualifications Test (SQT) is generally used as a means of evaluating the soldier's qualifications for the next higher grade. When a soldier, through no fault of his own, has not taken the SQT at the time he is to meet a promotion board, the Common Task Test (CTT) or a Commander's Evaluation (CE) can be considered as a means of judging the soldier's demonstrated qualifications for the next higher grade. An SQT score of 60 or higher is required to compete for promotion without a waiver; with a score of 59 or less, a waiver is required. The soldier who has no SQT score, through no fault of his own, does not need a waiver to compete for promotion. The no-waiver condition also applies to soldiers who have taken the SQT but have not yet received their score; to soldiers in an MOS for which no SQT has been developed or implemented into the promotion process (band members, for instance); and to soldiers who have been declared exempt from SQT evaluation by HQDA.

In addition to Skill Qualifications Test results, most soldiers meeting promotion boards for E5 or E6 must have completed Noncommissioned Officer Education System (NCOES) courses or on-the-job experience (OJE) requirements appropriate with their respective rank. (See the section on the *Noncommissioned Officer Education System* in chapter 2.)

A unique case exists for the soldier who is voluntarily or involuntarily reclassified to another primary MOS (PMOS). This soldier may not compete for promotions using SQT test results from the previous MOS. The soldier will be considered as having no SQT test results through no fault of his own.

SQT scores affect eligibility for promotion under very specific guidelines. First, test scores, when used, must be obtained from official documents: the most recent DA Form 2A, TSO data, or ISR. Test scores will be valid for 24 months unless replaced by a more recent test score. A soldier recommended for promotion—that is, placed on the recommended list by the promotion selection board—will not be removed from the list solely on receipt of his first SQT test results, even if the test score is less than 60. If, however, the soldier on the promotion list receives his second failing SQT test score, that soldier will be removed from the list unless a waiver is granted; the failing scores need not be consecutive scores. In addition, if two waivers have already been granted to that soldier, a third cannot be granted; the soldier will be removed from the local recommended promotion list.

Other Requirements for E5 or E6 Promotions

The time in service and time in grade requirements, and the SQT score requirements, are not the only factors affecting promotion eligibility. Beginning March 1987, a minimum education requirement for promotion to E5 and above will be high school graduation or GED equivalent. No waiver can be granted for this requirement. Further, once the new regulation is in effect, any soldier on the promotion list for E5 who does not meet the new requirement will be removed from the list. This change reflects an increased emphasis on raising educational standards among enlisted soldiers. Currently, higher education, at the associate degree level or above, is rewarded with extra points during the promotion board's review (see the *Meeting the Board* section in this chapter). If trends continue, future requirements for promotion for senior NCOs may include the associate degree as the minimum.

Certain MOSs require security clearances or security investigations. In such cases, regulations define levels of clearance required for each rank. Therefore, soldiers must meet the clearance requirements for the grade to which they wish to be promoted. In other words, no soldier can be promoted to E5 without already having the security clearance appropriate to that grade. No waiver can be granted for security clearances, although an interim clearance may be used if a full clearance is not yet available.

Physical qualifications are also required. Having a permanent physical profile does not restrict a soldier's promotion potential, provided the soldier has been reclassified into an MOS where he meets the physical demands of that occupational specialty. The physical qualifications requirement merely means that the soldier must be able to perform the duties of the MOS and grade for which he seeks promotion. Not meeting the Army's weight or body fat requirements, however, means that the soldier is not physically qualified for promotion.

A soldier may be disqualified for promotion based on "moral or administrative" reasons. These include having a court-martial conviction, being AWOL, or having lost time, if any of these occurred during the current term of enlistment. A waiver can be granted for these disqualifications, provided such a waiver would not mean the soldier had more than two waivers granted.

Waivers also may not be granted for the service-remaining obligation. To be promoted to E5, a soldier must have 3 months remaining before his

ETS. To be promoted to E6, the soldier must have 12 months remaining. Soldiers can extend or reenlist to meet the service-remaining obligation. If a bar to reenlistment or extension exists, the soldier without sufficient time remaining cannot be promoted.

A "position vacancy" at the next higher grade at a local unit is not required. Promotions to E5 and E6 are based on Army-wide needs.

Promotion Boards

Some general information on the makeup and governance of the promotion board may be helpful, but soldiers meeting a board for the first time are still advised to carefully read the *meeting the board* section in this chapter.

Promotion boards are convened on the fifteenth of each month in which soldiers have been recommended for promotion consideration. No prescreening boards can be held before the full promotion board to determine promotion eligibility. Boards will be conducted in a question and answer format.

Each board must have at least one member of the same sex as soldiers appearing before the board. In addition, at least one minority ethnic group must be represented on the board, whether or not any minority ethnic group soldiers are being considered for promotion during that month. No board can be made up entirely of servicemembers from minority ethnic groups, however.

Board members are appointed to the board by the promotion authority (a field grade officer responsible for promoting soldiers at a given command level). A president of the board must be appointed. If the president has voting authority, the voting members must be odd in number so that a tie can never occur. If the president does not have voting authority, he will serve as the tie-breaker in the event a tie vote should occur among voting members. All voting members and the president must be of a grade higher than the grade for which selections are being made. Boards can be made up of all officers (commissioned and warrant officers) or can be a mixture of enlisted and officer members. The senior member will preside over the board as the president of the board. Once a board is convened, each board member must be present to review every candidate for promotion.

A recorder is also a board member, but he has no voting authority. Consequently, the recorder does not have to be of a grade higher than the promotion grades being considered. Qualifications for the recorder include familiarity with Army personnel procedures. Ideally, the recorder should be from the organization's personnel and administration center (PAC) or from the Military Personnel Office (MILPO).

Every board member independently evaluates each soldier, using DA Form 3356. Members rate soldiers through a point system for six broad areas of evaluation:

- Personal appearance, bearing, and self-confidence.
- Oral expression and conversational skill.
- Knowledge of world affairs.
- Awareness of military programs.
- Knowledge of basic soldiering.
- Soldier's attitude, including leadership, potential for advancement, and trends in performance.

For each category, point spreads are given for soldiers rated as average, above average, excellent, and outstanding. The board members first decide which general rating the soldier merits, and then where in the allowable point spread to place the soldier. For instance, a soldier rated "excellent" on oral expression and conversational skill could be awarded 26 to 30. Once the board member had made the general "excellent" rating, he would have to refine that rating further with a numerical score within the spread allowable.

Total possible points for each soldier, from each individual board member, are 200 points. After all board members have evaluated the soldier, the recorder will pick up the forms, tally the vote from the section marked "do/do not recommend the soldier for promotion," and report the majority vote to the president. The president will break the tie if one exists. (The president of the board can cast only one vote; if the president is a regular voting member, there must be an odd number of voting members so that a tie cannot occur.) The recorder then averages the scores of the board (on DA Form 3357), so that the soldier is given a single composite score of not more than 200 from the board's evaluation.

Administrative points are also awarded and are entered on DA Form 3355 by the recorder; 800 administrative points are the maximum attainable. Administrative points are awarded for the following, listed in order of maximum points possible:

- Duty performance, as awarded by the soldier's commander through the promotion recommendation.
- SQT scores of 60 or above.
- Military education, including NCOES educational courses and

BOARD MEMBER APPRAISAL WORKSHEET
For use of this form, see AR 600-200; the proponent agency is MILPERCEN

NAME (Last, First, MI)	RECOMMENDED GRADE	PRESENT PMOS	RECOMMENDED CPMOS

BOARD INTERVIEW AND EVALUATION

AREAS OF EVALUATION	POINT SPREAD				TOTAL
	AVERAGE	ABOVE AVERAGE	EXCELLENT	OUTSTANDING	
1. PERSONAL APPEARANCE, BEARING AND SELF-CONFIDENCE	1-15 POINTS	16-20 POINTS	21-25 POINTS	26-30 POINTS	
2. ORAL EXPRESSION AND CONVERSATIONAL SKILL	1-15 POINTS	16-25 POINTS	26-30 POINTS	31-35 POINTS	
3. KNOWLEDGE OF WORLD AFFAIRS	1-10 POINTS	11-15 POINTS	16-20 POINTS	21-25 POINTS	
4. AWARENESS OF MILITARY PROGRAMS	1-10 POINTS	11-15 POINTS	16-20 POINTS	21-25 POINTS	
5. KNOWLEDGE OF BASIC SOLDIERING (Soldier's Manual). (See note)	1-15 POINTS	16-25 POINTS	26-35 POINTS	36-45 POINTS	
6. SOLDIER'S ATTITUDE (includes leadership and potential for advancement. Trends in performance, etc.).	1-15 POINTS	16-25 POINTS	26-35 POINTS	36-40 POINTS	
TOTAL POINTS AWARDED					
(MAXIMUM 200 POINTS)					

NOTE: Questions concerning the knowledge of basic soldiering will be tailored to include land navigation, survival, night operations, inclement weather operations, adverse environment and terrain.

REMARKS:

I DO_____ DO NOT _____ RECOMMEND THE SOLDIER FOR PROMOTION

RANK/SIGNATURE OF BOARD MEMBER	DATE

DA FORM 3356 MAR 85

EDITION OF NOV 80 IS OBSOLETE.

Board Member Appraisal Worksheet
(sample)

other military individual training courses (Ranger School, Special Forces Qualification courses, and correspondence courses).
- Military training, including PT test scores and marksmanship qualification.
- Civilian education.
- Awards and decorations.

Soldiers who are competing for promotions to E5 must attain a total score of 450, to be added to the list of recommended promotions, and they must be recommended by the majority of the board. Soldiers competing for promotions to E6 cannot be added to the list without a total score of 550. The recommended list for promotion will list soldiers by MOS, pay grade, and zone. Within appropriate groups, soldiers will be listed in descending order based on total points (the soldier with the most points within a given group will be listed first).

Promotions are made from the list. While orders can be issued with future effective dates, soldiers are not eligible for promotion until the first day of the third month following the date of selection. For example, soldiers meeting the board on January 15 are eligible for promotion on April 1.

Since cutoff points are established by HQDA separately for each zone, soldiers are transferred on the list from secondary zone to primary zone when they meet the necessary time in service requirements. On the first day of a soldier's thirty-third month of active duty, his name may be transferred from a secondary zone to a primary zone on the promotion list if the promotion being considered is for E5. Three months from then (the thirty-sixth month), the soldier is eligible for promotion. During the interim three months, the soldier's promotion would be based on the cutoff point for the secondary zone. Likewise, for promotion to E6, a soldier's name is moved from the secondary zone to the primary zone in his eighty-first month; he must still be considered under the point cutoff score for secondary zone until the first day of the eighty-fourth month, however.

Required Counseling

Each soldier who appears before a promotion selection board and is not recommended for promotion must be counseled. The individual with promotion authority may choose to counsel the soldier or may appoint another individual to do so. DA Forms 3355, 3356, and 3357, used by the board in its considerations, are to be employed in counseling the soldier. The counselor should point out ways in which the soldier can improve his promotion potential. After the counseling session, both the counselor and

DATA REQUIRED BY THE PRIVACY ACT OF 1974

AUTHORITY: Section 301, Title 5, USC.

PRINCIPAL PURPOSE: To determine eligibility for promotion.

ROUTINE USES: Information may be referred to appropriate authorities to determine promotion eligibility and validity of points granted.

DISCLOSURE: Voluntary, however, failure to furnish information requested may result in denial of promotion.

NAME	SOCIAL SECURITY NUMBER	RECOMMENDED GRADE
CURRENT ORGANIZATION	SRB/VRB MOS | PMOS	RECOMMENDED MOS

PART I — ADMINISTRATIVE POINTS (ITEMS 1—6)

1. ACTIVE FEDERAL SERVICE (AFS) — MAXIMUM 100 POINTS

A. Enter on line (1A) the number of months AFS required for board appearance in the recommended grade (primary zone):

	YEAR	MONTH	DAY
(1) Enter year and month in which board convenes. (1)			30
(2) Enter active Federal service date (see para 7-8b). (2)			
(3) To obtain creditable service for promotion purposes (3) subtract (2) from (1) to get (3). Enter total number of months on line (1B). (16 or more days will be credited as a whole month.)			+1

(1A) . . . . _____ (months)

= (1B) . . . . _____ (months)

B. Granted is 70 points for the required AFS. Add one point for each month the soldier's AFS exceeds line (1A). Subtract one point for each month that the soldier's AFS is less than (1A).

(1) If line (1B) is greater than line (1A), subtract line (1A) from line (1B) and enter the difference on line (1C). Add this difference to 70 to obtain promotion points granted.

(1C)____ plus 70 = _____

--OR--

(2) If line (1A) is greater than line (1B), subtract line (1B) from line (1A) and enter the difference on line (1D). Subtract the difference from 70 to obtain promotion points granted.

(1D) 70 minus___ = _____

POINTS GRANTED _____

2. TIME IN GRADE (TIMIG) — MAXIMUM 100 POINTS

A. Enter on line (2A) the months in present grade required for promotion to the next higher grade without waiver:

	YEAR	MONTH	DAY
(1) Enter year and month in which board convenes. (1)			30
(2) Enter soldier's Date of Rank (DOR). (2)			
(3) To obtain creditable TIMIG for promotion purposes, (3) subtract (2) from (1) to get (3). Enter total number of months on line (2B). (16 or more days will be credited as a whole month.)			+1

(2A) . . . . _____ (months)

= (2B) . . . . _____ (months)

B. Granted is 70 points for the required TIMIG. Add one point for each month the soldier's TIMIG exceeds line (2A). Subtract one point for each month that the soldier's TIMIG is less than line (2A).

(1) If line (2B) is greater than line (2A), subtract line (2A) from line (2B) and enter the difference on line (2C). Add this difference to 70 to obtain promotion points granted.

(2C)____ plus 70 = _____

--OR--

(2) If line (2A) is greater than line (2B), subtract line (2B) from line (2A) and enter the difference on line (2D). Subtract the difference from 70 to obtain promotion points granted.

(2D) 70 minus___ = _____

POINTS GRANTED _____

DA FORM **3355** NOV 80   EDITION OF 1 OCT 79 IS OBSOLETE.

Promotion Point Worksheet (page 1)
(sample)

3. DUTY PERFORMANCE — MAXIMUM 150 POINTS *(see note 6)*

A. For promotion to E-6: Enter Enlisted Evaluation Report Weighted Average *(EERWA)* on line *(3A)*. Use whole numbers - do not round fractions up. Grant promotion points indicated in table below.

(3A) . . . . _____

EERWA	PROMOTION POINTS	EERWA	PROMOTION POINTS	EERWA	PROMOTION POINTS
98 - below	=same as EERWA	107 - 108 =	124	117 - 118 =	139
99 - 100 =	112	109 - 110 =	127	119 - 120 =	142
101 - 102 =	115	111 - 112 =	130	121 - 122 =	145
103 - 104 =	118	113 - 114 =	133	123 - 124 =	148
105 - 106 =	121	115 - 116 =	136	125 =	150

B. For promotion to E-5: Enter points for Duty Performance based on DA Form 4187. *POINTS GRANTED* _____

4. SKILL QUALIFICATION TEST *(SQT)* — MAXIMUM 150 POINTS

A. Enter on line *(4A)* the soldier's latest "GO" raw SQT score from his/her Individual Soldier Report *(ISR)* or USAEREC Form 10A.

(4A) . . . . _____

B. Grant promotion points indicated in the table below. In those cases where soldiers are allowed to attain/retain list status without a verifying score *(less than 60)*, enter the "GO" Raw Score for points granted *(e.g., "GO" Raw Score of 56 = 56 promotion points)*.

POINTS GRANTED _____

PROMOTION POINTS		PROMOTION POINTS	
SQT SCORES =	*(Based on plus 1.5 points for each score)*	SQT SCORES =	*(Based on plus 3 points for each score)*
60 - 61 =	62	80 - 81 =	95
62 - 63 =	65	82 - 83 =	101
64 - 65 =	68	84 - 85 =	107
66 - 67 =	71	86 - 87 =	113
68 - 69 =	74	88 - 89 =	119
70 - 71 =	77	90 - 91 =	125
72 - 73 =	80	92 - 93 =	131
74 - 75 =	83	94 - 95 =	137
76 - 77 =	86	96 - 97 =	143
78 - 79 =	89	98 - 99 =	149
		100 =	150

--OR NO SQT DUE TO NO FAULT OF THE SOLDIER--

C. Soldiers authorized, IAW paragraph 7-15f, AR 600-200, to compete for promotion without SQT results will be awarded promotion points as follows:

(1) _____
(2) _____
(3) _____
(5) _____
(6) _____

(1) Enter and total the points awarded in Items 1, 2, 3, 5, and 6 of this form.

(2) Grant promotion points indicated in the table below.

(3) Grant 50 promotion points for all total administrative scores of 354 or below.

TOTAL _____

POINTS GRANTED _____

TOTAL SCORE	PRM POINTS	TOTAL SCORE	PRM POINTS	TOTAL SCORE	PRM POINTS	TOTAL SCORE	PRM POINTS
354 - below =	50	415 - 419 =	76	480 - 484 =	102	545 - 549 =	128
355 - 359 =	52	420 - 424 =	78	485 - 489 =	104	550 - 554 =	130
360 - 364 =	54	425 - 429 =	80	490 - 494 =	106	555 - 559 =	132
365 - 369 =	56	430 - 434 =	82	495 - 499 =	108	560 - 564 =	134
370 - 374 =	58	435 - 439 =	84	500 - 504 =	110	565 - 569 =	136
375 - 379 =	60	440 - 444 =	86	505 - 509 =	112	570 - 574 =	138
380 - 384 =	62	445 - 449 =	88	510 - 514 =	114	575 - 579 =	140
385 - 389 =	64	450 - 454 =	90	515 - 519 =	116	580 - 584 =	142
390 - 394 =	66	455 - 459 =	92	520 - 524 =	118	585 - 589 =	144
395 - 399 =	68	460 - 464 =	94	525 - 529 =	120	590 - 594 =	146
400 - 404 =	70	465 - 469 =	96	530 - 534 =	122	595 - 599 =	148
405 - 409 =	72	470 - 474 =	98	535 - 539 =	124	600 =	150
410 - 414 =	74	475 - 479 =	100	540 - 544 =	126		

DA FORM 3355

2

Promotion Point Worksheet (page 2)
(sample)

5. AWARDS AND DECORATIONS — MAXIMUM 50 POINTS

A. Enter in column (A) the number of awards received. Multiply (A) by the number of points authorized and enter in column (B). Total column (B) to determine promotion points granted *(see note 12).*

			(A)	(B)
(1)	Soldier's Medal or higher award	35	x _____	= _____
(2)	Bronze Star Medal *(Valor or Merit)*	30	x _____	= _____
(3)	Defense Meritorious Service Medal	25	x _____	= _____
(4)	Meritorious Service Medal	25	x _____	= _____
(5)	Air Medal *(Valor or Merit)*	20	x _____	= _____
(6)	Joint Service Commendation Medal	20	x _____	= _____
(7)	Army Commendation Medal *(Valor or Merit)*	20	x _____	= _____
(8)	Foreign Decoration *(Individual Award or Decoration)*	20	x _____	= _____
(9)	Purple Heart	15	x _____	= _____
(10)	Combat Infantry Badge	15	x _____	= _____
(11)	Combat Medical Badge	15	x _____	= _____
(12)	Good Conduct Medal	10	x _____	= _____
(13)	Expert Infantry Badge	10	x _____	= _____
(14)	Expert Field Medical Badge	10	x _____	= _____
(15)	Parachutist Badge	5	x _____	= _____
(16)	Divers Badge	5	x _____	= _____
(17)	Explosive Ordnance Disposal Badge *(Permanent awards only)*	5	x _____	= _____
(18)	Pathfinder Badge	5	x _____	= _____
(19)	Aircraft Crewman Badge *(Permanent awards only)*	5	x _____	= _____
(20)	Nuclear Reactor Operator Badge	5	x _____	= _____
(21)	Ranger Tab	5	x _____	= _____
(22)	Driver and Mechanic Badge	5	x _____	= _____
(23)	Air Assault Badge	5	x _____	= _____
(24)	Drill Sergeant Identification Badge	5	x _____	= _____
(25)	US Army Recruiter Badge	5	x _____	= _____
(26)	Expert Marksmanship Qualification Badge *(Most recent score on individual weapon only — Limit 5 points)*	5	x _____	= _____
(27)	Campaign Star *(Battle Star)*	5	x _____	= _____
(28)	Certificate of Achievement *(DA Form 2442) (See memo in MPRJ)* and locally designed certificates *(Awarded by commanders serving in positions authorized the rank of LTC (O5) or higher — Limit 10 points) (See action pending section MPRJ)*	5	x _____	= _____

POINTS GRANTED _____

B. Equivalent awards and decorations earned in other US Uniformed Forces receive same points as Army Awards.

6. INDIVIDUAL TRAINING AND CIVILIAN EDUCATION — MAXIMUM 200 POINTS

A. INDIVIDUAL TRAINING: Grant points as follows:

		PROMOTION POINTS
(1)	Noncommissioned Officer Education System (NCOES) *(see note 5)*	
(a)	Primary level *(only applies if recommended for E5)*	PNCOC/CA - 30 PLC - 30 PTC - 30

- - - OR - - -

| (b) | Basic level *(only applies if recommended for E6)* | BNCOC/CA - 30
PLC - 30
BTC - 30 |

- - - OR - - -

| (c) | Certification of OJE by Commander IAW AR 351-1 *(applies only for soldiers who do not qualify for points for NCOES courses under (a) and (b) above and who have a PMOS for which SQT is used for promotion).* | OJE - 15 points for basic certification. Award 1 additional point *(not to exceed 15)* for each month the soldier meets the position requirement for OJE *(see AR 351-1).* See Note 11. |

| (2) | All other courses successfully completed of at least one week duration. *(See notes 1, 2, 3, 4 and 5).* | - 2 points per week |

| (3) | Correspondence *(extension)* subcourses, satisfactorily completed *(see note 9).* | - 1 point per 5 credit hours |

DA FORM 3355   3

Promotion Point Worksheet (page 3)
(sample)

B. Annotate all individual training courses and date completed with points awarded. *(Continue on back of page 5 if additional space is needed.)*

_____
_____
_____
_____

C. Enter on line *(6A)* the total promotion points awarded for Individual Training.   *(6A)* . . . . . . _____

D. CIVILIAN EDUCATION: Grant points as indicated below.
   (1) High School:

YEAR COMPLETED	PROMOTION POINTS
8-below	0
9	15
10	30
11	45
12	60
High School Diploma/GED	75

   (2) Business/Trade School/College: Grant 1 point for each semester hour earned *(see notes 7, 8 and 10).*

E. Annotate all civilian education courses with points awarded. *(Continue on back of page 5 if additional space is needed.)*

_____
_____
_____
_____

F. Enter on line *(6B)* the total promotion points awarded for Civilian Education.   *(6B)* . . . . . . _____

G. Total lines *(6A)* and *(6B)*.   POINTS GRANTED _____

THE ABOVE ADMINISTRATIVE POINTS SHOWN HAVE BEEN ACCURATELY EXTRACTED FROM
APPROPRIATE RECORDS AND PROMOTION LIST POINTS INDICATED ARE CORRECT.

DATE	SIGNATURE OF RESPONSIBLE OFFICIAL	SIGNATURE OF RECOMMENDED INDIVIDUAL

PART II - TOTAL

7. TOTAL ADMINISTRATIVE POINTS - MAXIMUM 750 POINTS

GRANTED _____

8. TOTAL BOARD POINTS - MAXIMUM 250 POINTS

GRANTED _____

9. TOTAL PROMOTION POINTS - MAXIMUM 1,000 POINTS

NOTE - Only the fractional total promotion points in Item 9 will be rounded off to the nearest whole number. A fraction of 5/10 or higher will be rounded up to the next higher whole number. A fraction of 4/10 or less will be rounded down to the next lowest whole number.

GRANTED _____

THE TOTAL POINTS SHOWN HAVE BEEN ACCURATELY EXTRACTED FROM APPROPRIATE
RECORDS AND PROMOTION LIST POINTS INDICATED ARE CORRECT.

DATE	SIGNATURE OF BOARD RECORDER

DA FORM 3355   4

Promotion Point Worksheet (page 4)
(sample)

the soldier must sign DA Form 3355, which is then filed with the complete board proceedings.

Reevaluation and Recomputation of Points

Even after the soldier is on the promotion list, he may request a reevaluation if his administrative points have increased by at least 50 points. The increase in points must be from a higher SQT score (or CTT or CE if the SQT was not available); additional awards or decorations; or increases in military or civilian education, or in military training. Soldiers requesting reevaluation may elect to appear before the board, but they are not required to do so.

Appearing before the board could either increase or decrease the board points, because a new evaluation of the soldier by the board is completely independent of the previous evaluation. Before requesting a reevaluation, a soldier must sign a statement indicating he understands that the evaluation by the new board is final; and that if the new board does not recommend promotion, or awards fewer board points so that the soldier no longer meets promotion cutoff points, he will then be removed from the promotion list.

The soldier who elects not to appear before the board will have his administrative points adjusted and will be eligible for promotion using the higher point total on the first day of the third month after reevaluation. During the interim period, the soldier can still be promoted based on the previous point score.

When administrative points are increased by less than 50 points, a soldier may still request reevaluation if he has been on the list for a minimum of six months. Under these circumstances, however, it is mandatory that the soldier appear before the board a second time. The same criteria apply: the soldier can be removed from the list if not recommended for promotion by the board, or if the board awards fewer points and the soldier then does not meet cutoff point requirements.

Soldiers removed from the promotion list through reevaluation can be considered for promotion by future boards. Such consideration is processed in the same manner as the initial evaluation—initiated through the commander's recommendation.

Placement on a promotion list does not necessarily mean a quick promotion is ahead. Soldiers may be on the list for more than a year before being promoted. Under such cases, administrative points are recalculated annually without request by the soldier and without action by the board. Soldiers review the recomputation for accuracy and completeness. New scores are added to the next published promotion list and, like initial scores, become effective three months after being updated on the list. In the interim the soldier can be promoted based on the old score.

Promotions under Unusual Circumstances

Once on the promotion list, a soldier may still be promoted while on TDY or on special duty or assignment. The commander of the unit to which the soldier is attached temporarily must verify the soldier's eligibility before promoting him. The promotion is not to be withheld simply because the soldier is not at his regularly assigned duty station.

Likewise, soldiers reassigned prior to promotion, who are already on the promotion list, are to be added to the promotion list at the new assignment based on the board recommendation from the previous assignment. No board action is required for this transaction.

If a soldier becomes eligible for promotion to E5 or E6 by meeting the cutoff point score while in transit between assignments, he will be promoted at the new assignment by the promoting authority there. This differs somewhat for promotions to E2 through E4; these soldiers are promoted by the Commander, MILPERCEN, if they meet eligibility, without waiver, while in transit status.

Commanders of local medical facilities will promote soldiers hospitalized with serious illnesses or injuries received in the line of duty when those soldiers become eligible to be promoted from the recommended list. This ruling applies to E3s who are recommended by their unit commanders for promotion to E4, as well as to E4s and E5s on the list for promotion to E5 or E6, respectively.

Nonpromotable Status

Promotions are important to the soldier's career and morale. The fact that a soldier has received a commander's recommendation for promotion, or has been placed on a promotion list for E5 or E6, does not guarantee promotion. Under certain circumstances, the soldier can move into a nonpromotable status. No promotion will then be made, regardless of previous decisions, until the soldier has been removed from the nonpromotable status.

A soldier becomes nonpromotable when he:

- Is AWOL.
- Is in civilian or military confinement (placed under arrest or in a jail).
- Has deserted.

- Is ill or injured *not in the line of duty.*
- Is under court-martial charges.
- Is serving a court-martial sentence, including a suspended sentence.
- Is undergoing proceedings that may result in other than honorable discharge.
- Has received a Report for Suspension of Favorable Personnel Actions (DA form 268).
- Is being considered for a DA Form 268 by an officer having general court-martial (or higher) authority.
- Is recommended for reclassification due to inefficiency or disciplinary reasons. (A letter must be sent to the promotion authority under this condition before the soldier is nonpromotable.)
- Is being punished under Article 15, even if the punishment is suspended.
- Is not qualified for reenlistment.
- Cannot receive an appropriate security clearance or favorable security investigation for the promotion grade for which he is being considered.
- Is recommended for a reduction to a lower grade. (A letter must be sent to the promotion authority before the soldier is nonpromotable; then the promotion authority must decide whether to convene a board to consider the reduction in grade.)
- Fails to take the SQT test through his own fault.
- Does not have necessary qualifications or formal training required for his career specialty.
- Exceeds the Army weight standards or the body fat requirements.
- Fails the PT test, but does not have a medical exemption such as a physical profile.
- Has not taken the PT test during the past nine months (exceptions are made for circumstances beyond the control of the individual).

Removal from nonpromotable status is usually obvious. It occurs when confinement ends; the court-martial sentence or Article 15 punishment is completed; proceedings against the soldier are completed but do not result in a discharge; Army weight and body fat requirements are met; or necessary tests, clearances, or qualifications are achieved.

A few conditions for removal from nonpromotable status are not as obvious. Reports for Suspension of Favorable Personnel Actions contain an effective time frame; when the suspension is over, the soldier is again promotable. Soldiers being reclassified must compete under their new MOS classification; the nonpromotable status applies to the old MOS specialty. Soldiers failing to take the SQT test through their own fault are again promotable once they take the test; if, however, the test is no longer available for their MOS, these soldiers may have to wait up to one year before regaining promotable status.

Acting NCOs

Under special circumstances a unit commander may wish to promote a soldier to an Acting NCO. When NCO positions are vacant at the company, troop, battery, or detachment units, the commander may find it expeditious to promote junior soldiers to fill these positions. Individuals cannot be promoted to Acting NCO if they are more than one pay grade below the rank into which they are being promoted; an E3, for instance, could not be promoted to an Acting Sergeant (E5).

Acting NCOs generally wear the regular insignia associated with the rank. The rank is to be affixed permanently to the soldier's uniform under the same rules governing rank insignia for all soldiers. Use of special Acting NCO brassards is discouraged.

While the Acting NCO has all of the authority of a regularly appointed NCO of the same grade, he continues to receive pay and allowances at the lower level. In addition, time spent in the Acting NCO rank will not count toward time in grade at the higher rank; it will count as time in grade at the lower rank.

It should be noted that promotion to Acting NCO is a positive contribution to the soldier's career progression. Demonstrated leadership qualities are favorably considered when the soldier is eligible for promotion to the higher rank.

ENLISTED EVALUATION REPORT

No other document affects your career as heavily as DA Form 2166-6, the Enlisted Evaluation Report (EER). EERs are prepared for all enlisted soldiers in grades E5 and above. Their purpose is to evaluate your duty performance, professionalism, and advancement potential. Through this singular document the senior enlisted leadership for the Army is determined and developed. The EER is used in conjunction with your other qualifications and the needs of the Army to determine a broad spectrum of actions directly influencing your career. Among these actions are promotions, school selections, MOS classifications, and future assignments.

Understanding the criteria used in the evaluation and the process through which the evaluation is conducted and reviewed can help you be better prepared for the EER so that this document will be as positive an influence on your career as possible. The basic areas evaluated are daily performance of duties, professionalism as a soldier, and personal traits. These areas include your weaknesses as well as your strengths, abilities, and potential.

According to AR 623-205 the EER is designed to be comprehensive, accurate, complete, thoughtful, and fair in its appraisal. The narrative section of the report is every bit as important as the numerical score given. From that section you can learn most vividly where and how you can improve performance to enhance future EERs. The general philosophy is *not* one of expecting perfection from each servicemember, but rather a philosophy of *continuous* professional development and growth.

The evaluation report process should include counseling by the evaluator on career development. This vital link in the process is the best means of your increasing your understanding of what is expected of you. Ideally, counseling should not only *follow* the EER report, but should also *precede* it, allowing ample time for you to improve areas identified as weaknesses. An indorser and reviewer are involved in the process as a means of keeping the EER as objective as possible. In the event you disagree with the evaluation, an appeal process is available.

The chain of command/supervision is the most common model for the rating chain. Indeed, by AR 623-205, the rating chain should correspond as nearly as possible to the chain of command within the organization. The rating chain is also required to be published and posted within the unit, by name or duty position, so that each soldier knows in advance who will be his rater, indorser, and reviewer. In addition, the regulation itself must be made available to any soldier who requests it.

The process then is to include advance notice of evaluators, timely job performance counseling, career development counseling, a fair and complete evaluation, review of the evaluation by two individuals above the rater in the chain of command, and assistance in preparing and filing an appeal if the soldier so requests.

Time Limitations

A minimum rating period of three months has been established. This means that a soldier must have worked directly for the rater for that minimum time period before the rater is qualified to evaluate the soldier. Certain time periods, when the soldier is not under the supervision of the rater, are excluded as "nonrated periods." Among the nonrated periods are time spent in transit between duty stations, including any TDY assignments, leave, or travel time between stations; time spent as a patient in a

ENLISTED EVALUATION REPORT
(AR 623-205)

Proponent agency for this form is the US
Army Military Personnel Center.

PART I. ADMINISTRATIVE DATA

A. LAST NAME — FIRST NAME — MIDDLE INITIAL		B. SSN	C. RANK (ABBR)	D. DATE OF RANK

E. PRIMARY MOSC	F. SECONDARY MOSC	G. UNIT, ORGANIZATION, STATION, ZIP CODE/APO, MACOM

H. CODE/TYPE OF REPORT	I. PERIOD OF REPORT					J. RATED MONTHS	K. NONRATED MONTHS	L. NONRATED CODES
	FROM	YEAR	MONTH	THRU	YEAR	MONTH			

PART II. DUTY DESCRIPTION

A. PRINCIPAL DUTY TITLE:	B. DUTY MOSC:

C. DESCRIPTION OF DUTIES:

PART III. EVALUATION OF PROFESSIONALISM AND PERFORMANCE

RATER	INDORSER	A. PROFESSIONAL COMPETENCE	SCORING SCALE	RATER	INDORSER	B. PROFESSIONAL STANDARDS
		1. Demonstrates initiative.	(High)			1. Integrity.
		2. Adapts to changes.				2. Loyalty.
		3. Seeks self-improvement.	5			3. Moral courage.
		4. Performs under pressure.	4			4. Self-discipline.
		5. Attains results.				5. Military appearance.
		6. Displays sound judgment.	3			6. Earns respect.
		7. Communicates effectively.	2			7. Supports EO/EEO.
		8. Develops subordinates.	1			SUBTOTALS
		9. Demonstrates technical skills.	0			
		10. Physical fitness.	(Low)			[Add the Rater's SUBTOTALS (A&B) and enter sum in the appropriate box in PART VI, SCORE SUMMARY. Do the same for Indorser.]
		SUBTOTALS				

C. DEMONSTRATED PERFORMANCE OF PRESENT DUTY

1. Rater's Evaluation:

2. Indorser's Evaluation:

DA FORM 2166-6 OCT 81   REPLACES DA FORM 2166-5A, OCT 79, WHICH IS OBSOLETE.

Enlisted Evaluation Report (front)
(sample)

PART IV. EVALUATION OF POTENTIAL

1. Rater's Evaluation: (Place score in applicable box)

40-38	37-20	19-0	40-0
☐ Promote ahead of peers.	☐ Promote with peers.	☐ Do not promote.	☐ E9 Soldiers Only.

Comments. (potential for higher-level school, assignment, and supervisory responsibility)

2. Indorser's Evaluation: (Place score in applicable box)

40-38	37-20	19-0	40-0
☐ Promote ahead of peers.	☐ Promote with peers.	☐ Do not promote.	☐ E9 Soldiers Only.

Comments: (potential for higher-level school, assignment, and supervisory responsibility)

PART V. AUTHENTICATION

A. NAME OF RATER (Last, First, MI)	SSN	SIGNATURE

RANK, ORGANIZATION, AND DUTY ASSIGNMENT	DATE

Refer to AR 623-205 for requirements to discuss contents of report with the rated soldier.

B. NAME OF INDORSER (Last, First, MI)	SSN	SIGNATURE

RANK, ORGANIZATION, AND DUTY ASSIGNMENT	DATE

C. NAME OF RATED SOLDIER (Last, First, MI)	I have verified Administrative Data, PART I, and Duty Description, PART II. I have seen this report as prepared by the Rater and Indorser. I understand that my signature does not constitute agreement nor disagreement with their evaluations.

SSN	DATE	Signature:

D. NAME OF REVIEWER (Last, First, MI)	SSN	I have reviewed this report in accordance with

RANK, ORGANIZATION, AND DUTY ASSIGNMENT

AR 623-205 on _____ (date)

Signature:

PART VI. SCORE SUMMARY

PART	RATER SCORE	INDORSER SCORE
III.		
IV.		
Sum		
REPORT SCORE (R + I ÷ 2) =		

PART VII. MILPO CERTIFICATION

A. SOLDIER'S COPY:

☐ Given to Soldier _____ (date)

☐ Forwarded to Soldier _____ (date)

☐ Mailed to Soldier _____ (date)

B. FORWARDING ADDRESS:

C. NO. OF INCL	D. DATE ENTERED ON DA FORM 2-1	E. MILPO SIGNATURE	F. MILPO CODE

Enlisted Evaluation Report (back)
(sample)

hospital or on convalescent leave; time spent in military or civilian schools; TDYs or special duties that take the soldier away from his normal work assignment; and less desirable nonrated periods for time spent as a prisoner of war, missing in action, AWOL or desertion status, or confined in a military or civilian detention or correction facility. The EER must account for all time, chronologically, with special codes entered on the EER for each of the nonrated periods listed above.

EERs are normally submitted annually, 12 months after promotion to E5, or 12 months after the last report. *Special reports* are submitted when the situation demands it—either on a positive or negative basis. When a soldier's conduct is so outstanding, or so deficient, that the rater believes that the situation should be handled through a special EER, he may submit one before the normal 12-month period. A special EER may be used to recognize a soldier for some outstanding act or deed, or for a period of highly exemplary service. Further, with the special EER the minimum rating period is reduced from 3 months to 30 days.

The special report must be approved by the reviewer, based on the outstanding nature of service or deed. If it is not approved, the report, stating the reason for disapproval, will be returned through the indorser to the rater. A special report cannot be issued simply to help the soldier who is in a primary or secondary zone of consideration for promotion or school selection. The rated soldier must be informed of any disapproved report, and the report must then be destroyed.

An additional requirement for the special evaluation report is that it be approved by the first O6 (full colonel) or general officer in the soldier's chain of command. If this officer is not in the normal reviewer/indorser chain, he may act as both reviewer and indorser for the special EER.

Several circumstances require additional EERs. *Change-of-rater reports* are submitted when the rater retires, dies, or is relieved; when the soldier's expiration of term of service (ETS) occurs, unless he has immediately reenlisted with no break in service; when the soldier is serving on special assignment or TDY, outside of the supervision of the normal rater, for a period of 90 days or more; or when the soldier is in a military or civilian school for a period of 90 days or more (school evaluations are made on an *academic evaluation report*—AER).

Complete-the-record reports can also be submitted under special circumstances, although these evaluations are optional. When a soldier is in the primary or secondary zone of consideration for a Department of the Army centralized promotion board, or is being considered for selection to a military or civilian school, and has not yet been rated for his current duty assignment but has been in that assignment for at least six months, the rater may submit a complete-the-record report so that the soldier's personnel file is up-to-date before the board's review.

Relief-for-cause reports are submitted when a soldier is removed from his assignment because "personal or professional characteristics, conduct, behavior, or performance of duty warrant removal in the best interest of the US Army" (AR 600-20, para. 3-13). Relief from duty must be preceded by counseling by the rater, allowing the soldier time to correct deficiencies. Temporary suspension from assigned duties does not warrant a relief-for-cause report. The narrative portion of such a report must clearly define the reasons for the action taken and must specify that the soldier has been notified of the reasons. Minimum rating period is 30 days, although this minimum can be waived by a general officer or an officer with courts-martial authority over the soldier; cases in which such a waiver would be considered are only those cases where clear-cut misconduct is evident and warrants such action.

Information an EER Cannot Include

Since the EER has such wide-ranging influence on your career, restrictions have been placed on types of information that can be included. For instance, if a soldier voluntarily enrolls in the ADAPCP program for alcohol or drug abuse, that information cannot be included in subsequent EERs. This does not mean that poor performance due to the alcohol or drug problems cannot be noted in the evaluation. On the other hand, if the supervisor identifies the problem and requires the soldier's entrance into the program, the soldier can then be identified in the EER as having the problem. Such identification must be based on information obtained from sources outside of the ADAPCP program. Once a soldier has been so identified in an EER, subsequent evaluations should highlight successful rehabilitation as a positive credit to the soldier.

The servicemember is protected from the inclusion of unproven derogatory information in an EER. This pertains to investigations or legal proceedings that have not been completed and to criminal accusations that resulted in a not-guilty verdict. Further, no unfavorable comments are allowed in an EER concerning the zeal with which a soldier performs duties such as the Equal Opportunity NCO or counsel to the accused in a court-martial.

Comments related to the soldier's race, color, religion, sex, or national origin are also considered to be inappropriate. In addition, no mention can be made of the fact that a soldier received an Article 15; the misconduct that resulted in the Article 15 can, however, be noted.

The Appeal Process

When you disagree with an EER, you may take one of two actions: request a commander's inquiry or begin an appeal. The first, technically, is not an appeal, but rather a direct request—by the soldier or by another individual aware of an unfair or unjust evaluation of a soldier—that the commander investigate an inaccurate evaluation *before* it becomes a matter of permanent record. Such inquiries are limited to problems with the clarity of the report, information presented as facts in the report, conduct of the rated soldier and the rater during the evaluation process, and compliance with regulations governing EERs. Commander inquiries may not be used to document difference in opinion between the rater and the reviewer or indorser with regard to the soldier's performance or potential, or between the commander and the rating officials. The evaluation of the rating chain is considered to be the organization's view of the rated soldier.

Through the commander's inquiry, you have a means of redress before the EER is accepted as an official evaluation. The commander's inquiry is used when serious irregularities or errors exist in the evaluation process or in the evaluation itself. Many types of injustices could prompt a soldier to request a commander's inquiry. Among them would be a lack of objectivity or fairness by either the rater or reviewers, untrue or inaccurate statements made in the EER, or failure by the rater/reviewer to follow the proper administrative process in evaluating the soldier. Instances of improper process could be an unqualified official, one who had not been supervisor of the soldier for the minimum time period, for instance, or one who had himself been under some type of investigation, which had been substantiated, for improper conduct.

Use of the commander's inquiry is not necessarily the first step in the appeal process, although it is often used as such. Nor does use of the commander's inquiry eliminate the possibility of a soldier beginning an appeal if he is not satisfied with the results of the requested inquiry. In other words, the two processes—the commander's inquiry and the appeal process—are separate, distinct procedures. In addition, invoking one process places no limitations on beginning the next, but the first process is not a prerequisite for the second.

EERs and AERs are presumed to be correct when accepted through official channels of the military personnel system. The appeal process exists so that you can correct, or attempt to correct, evaluations you believe to be in error. The Army recognizes that an unfair or unjust evaluation hurts not only the soldier involved but also the interests of the Army itself, since so many career and leadership decisions are molded by the evaluations of individual soldiers. The Army is not, however, capricious in calling into question the integrity and fairness of the rating officials. It becomes the responsibility of the soldier to show *beyond doubt* that there is sufficient cause to question the judgment of the rating officials.

The appeal process handles two basic types of problems: administrative-type corrections to an EER and substantive corrections—appeals claiming injustice, bias, prejudice, or inaccurate evaluations. In both cases the burden of proof lies with the appellant. In most cases, the appellant is the rated soldier; another individual, however, may make the appeal on behalf of the rated soldier, but only with the soldier's concurrence, which must be documented with other evidence submitted. A rating official may not initiate an appeal after reconsidering the evaluation he has submitted. Nor may a rating official submit an appeal based on typographical errors or administrative oversight. The appeal process calls into question some of these very factors, but it must be initiated by an individual other than the rater, reviewer, or indorser.

No time limitations exist on the filing of an appeal. As more time elapses between the evaluation and the appeal, however, it becomes increasingly difficult to document errors, especially errors in judgment. Normally, if an appeal is initiated five years or more after an evaluation, it is very difficult to reconstruct the soldier's performance with enough evidence to change an evaluation. It should be noted here that establishing judgment error is not easy, even shortly after it has occurred. The longer the soldier waits before attempting to prove the error, the more difficult the task becomes.

Administrative errors are the easiest to prove. Often they involve data recorded elsewhere. A published rating chain could be used to show that the proper supervisory official was not involved in the evaluation. Assignment orders, TDY orders, or travel orders could be used to show that the minimum time period was not completed before the evaluation was made; hospitalization or leave records could also be used to document the same. Extracts from unit morning reports, personnel data card entries, or statements from military personnel officers (or other individuals who would have knowledge of the situation) could also be submitted as evidence of administrative error. Basically, *any* document that has bearing on the point in question can be submitted as evidence.

Substantive errors—those errors in accuracy, judgment, or fairness—are much more difficult to prove. There are no records or documents that show prejudice or bias. Such claims are based for the most part on evidence from third parties—persons other than the rater or the soldier being rated, who have knowledge of the soldier's performance during the rating period in question. Ideally, this individual should be someone who had opportunity to view the soldier firsthand, to observe his performance and the interaction between the soldier and the rater. Statements are acceptable from individuals who could not have observed firsthand, but they are not as strong. Such statements may be included when the individual has knowledge of the circumstances, factual error, erroneous perceptions or judgment, or existing bias or prejudice on the part of the rater.

Any statement submitted as evidence of injustice should be as specific as possible. Generalized accounts with no factual data carry little weight with an appeals board. In addition, statements about the soldier's previous performance in periods not covered by the evaluation report, or his subsequent performance after the period covered by the report, are of little value. The statements must deal directly with the time period in question. A possible exception occurs when a statement can be provided with regard to the soldier's performance prior to the rating period when the soldier was performing the same types of duties in the same unit under similar circumstances. Letters of commendation or appreciation, and citations at the end of a tour also provide only limited evidence in support of the appeal, even if such documents covered the rating period. In addition, statements regarding the soldier's future value to the Army carry little weight in appealing an evaluation. Also, little evidence of an unjust evaluation is provided by a statement attesting to personality conflict between the rater and the rated soldier, unless such a statement can show conclusively that the conflict resulted in a biased or inaccurate appraisal of the soldier's performance.

Then what types of statements are of value? How can the soldier prove convincingly that indeed the evaluation was inaccurate or unjust? First, evidence must be based on statements from more than one person. While volume is not the key ingredient to a successful appeal, it is crucial that more than one "third party" disagree with the evaluation. Individuals with various perspectives of the circumstances involved form the most convincing group. A subordinate's opinion of the soldier's performance is not valid evidence of erroneous judgment by the rater. Statements from the rating officials themselves can be included as evidence, if they address factual errors, erroneous judgments, or bias. Such statements should include specific details as to how such errors occurred, explaining the circumstances leading to the errors. Simply stating that the rating official has changed his opinion of the soldier's performance is not a strong statement.

Filing the Appeal

An appeal can be made contesting either the full evaluation report or only specific parts of the comments included. All evidence submitted must be relevant to the claim made in the appeal. Documents must be either originals or certified true copies of originals. Statements should be made in duplicate and must clearly identify the third party's relationship to the soldier during the time period in question. They should address only those aspects of the evaluation that the soldier is appealing. Sworn statements are the most convincing; the JAG Office can be of assistance in obtaining such statements and in advising the soldier during the appeal process.

The actual appeal is made in the form of a military letter, also submitted in duplicate. Signing and dating the appeal letter is critical. The report being appealed should be included, in duplicate, and again the original or a certified true copy is to be sent. Certified true copies of the soldier's DA Form 2A and DA Form 2-1 from the military personnel jacket should also be included, in duplicate.

In collecting the evidence, the soldier should bear in mind that the appeals board participants will have no personal knowledge of the circumstances or individuals involved and will base their opinion solely on documents submitted. The burden of proof can sometimes seem overwhelming, often resulting in the soldier not being fully satisfied with the evidence obtained. The soldier is cautioned however, not to procrastinate in the filing of the appeal, since time can erode the credibility of the evidence submitted. Prompt submission of an appeal is in the soldier's best interest.

The soldier should also be aware that he cannot invalidate an entire EER or AER by proving that a minor administrative error was made. Further, proving that one rating official's evaluation was unjust does not invalidate the evaluations of the other two rating officials involved.

Appeals and all supporting documentation should be submitted to:

> Commander
> U.S. Army Enlisted Records
>   and Evaluation Center
> ATTN: PCRE-RE-A
> Ft. Benjamin Harrison, IN 46249-5301

If the appeal is denied, the soldier will be notified and the letter of notification will be included on the soldier's performance microfiche. Other correspondence related to a denied appeal will be placed on the soldier's restricted fiche. If an appeal is returned because of insufficient evidence, however, it is not recorded in the soldier's permanent record.

Once an appeal has been denied, the soldier has two recourses. Additional evidence can be submitted and an appeal can be reconsidered. If this action results in a denial of the appeal, the soldier can then request action be taken by the Army Board for Correction of Military Records, consulting AR 15-185 as a guide to such a request.

5

Moving On

Moving is a part of the military lifestyle. Travel within the United States and overseas is often considered a major benefit of military service. New sights, foreign customs, and another adventure are rarely more than three years away.

ENLISTED PERSONNEL ASSIGNMENT SYSTEM

Where you live and work is determined by the Army's Enlisted Personnel Assignment System. The principal goal of the assignment system is to meet personnel requirements for the Army. The needs of the Army must come first. Through the assignment system, however, the Army also strives to accomplish several goals for its soldiers.

First, recognizing that all assignments are not equally desirable, the system aims at equalizing desirable and undesirable assignments by reassigning the "most eligible" soldier from each rank and MOS group. In this manner, a fair distribution of the assignments is most likely. Further, the hardships of military life (the undesirable assignments) also get a fair distribution among the soldiers.

The personal desires of individual soldiers (as indicated on DA Form 2635—Enlisted Preference Statement) are also considered, but they are not of primary concern in making assignments.

A final and important consideration of the assignment system is providing all soldiers with the best opportunities for professional development and advancement potential through varied assignments.

How does the system work? First, Military Personnel Offices (MILPOs) submit requisitions, stating the number of personnel needed and the requirements for each (MOS and grade), to the Military Personnel Center (MILPERCEN). The requisitions are based on the station's projected gains and losses in personnel. MILPERCEN then compares its lists of available soldiers to the requisitions.

Soldiers become available for reassignment when they are awarded an initial or a new MOS; when they volunteer for reassignment; when they complete schooling or training; or when they complete an overseas tour, a stabilization period, or the normal "turn-around time" in CONUS. (Each MOS has an established period that is considered "normal" for a soldier to spend stateside before being assigned an additional overseas position.)

Available soldiers are matched against requisitions based on their grade, MOS, and skill level, and their current ETS. In addition, Skill Qualification Identifiers (SQI) and Additional Skill Identifiers (ASI) are considered. The number of months since the last PCS and the number of months since serving in an overseas assignment are other major considerations, as is the soldier's availability month compared to the requirement month. Finally, the soldier's area of preference is considered. It should be noted, however, that the preference of the individual soldier can only be honored if the needs of the Army are also served by making the desired assignment. Scores are devised based on these criteria, and then the scores are used in making the final assignment decisions.

When an assignment is likely to cause severe family hardship, the soldier can request a deferment or deletion from the assignment. Most extreme problems are further complicated when the move is to be to a dependent-restricted overseas assignment. (Deferments and deletions are discussed fully later in this chapter.)

Soldiers can also request an early arrival. Requests should be made directly to MILPERCEN (DAPC-EPS-S) when the soldier has been assigned to a short-tour overseas area; when the request is for an early arrival in excess of 60 days; or when the need for the request occurs while the soldier is TDY or en route to the new assignment. Requests for early arrivals of less than 60 days can be approved by the installation commander at the soldier's current assignment if the upcoming assignment is to a long-term overseas area.

ENLISTED PREFERENCE STATEMENT

For use of this form, see AR 614-200; the proponent agency is MILPERCEN.

SEE REVERSE SIDE FOR INSTRUCTIONS.

BEFORE COMPLETING THIS FORM SEE REVERSE FOR DATA REQUIRED BY THE PRIVACY ACT.

SECTION I - IDENTIFICATION AND CLASSIFICATION DATA

1. NAME	2. SOCIAL SECURITY NO.	3. GRADE		4. MOS				
		PROM IND	ABBR	a. PMOSC	ASI	b. SMOSC	ASI	

5. DUTY		6. DROS/ DEROS	7. ARRIVAL DATE CURR ORG	8. CURRENT ORGANIZATION	9. UNIT PROCESS-ING CODE	10. YR & MO LAST PCS
MOSC	ASI					

SECTION II - CURRENT CONUS AND OVERSEA ASSIGNMENT PREFERENCE AND AEA CODE

11a. CURR O/S AREA OF PREF		b. CURRENT CONUS AREA OF PREFERENCE		c. AEA *		
AREA	CODE	AREA	CODE	CODE	TERMINATION YR & MO	*See Item 3b of Instructions on Reverse Side.*

SECTION III - REQUESTED CONUS AND OVERSEA ASSIGNMENT PREFERENCE
(List area of preference for next assignment in order of priority by number)

12a. PRIMARY OVERSEA AREA OF PREFERENCE		b. PRIMARY CONUS AREA PREFERENCE	
AREA	CODE	AREA	CODE

13. NO.	LONG TOUR AREA	CODE	NO.	SHORT TOUR AREA	CODE	NO.	CONUS ARMY AREA-STATION	CODE
						2		
						3		
						4		
						5		
						6		

SECTION IV - DUTY ASSIGNMENT PREFERENCE

14.
☐ RECRUITING/CAREER COUNSELOR * ☐ DRILL SERGEANT ☐ FIRST SERGEANT ☐ RESERVE COMPONENT DUTY
☐ SERVICE SCHOOL INSTRUCTOR ☐ MAAG - MISSION * ☐ TROOPS ☐ STAFF ☐ ROTC DUTY
*See Item 3c of Instructions on Reverse Side

15. MILITARY SCHOOL PREFERENCE *(DA PAM 351-4)*

SECTION V - MISCELLANEOUS

16. UPON COMPLETION OF MY CURRENT OVERSEA TOUR AN INTERTHEATER TRANSFER IS DESIRED
☐ YES ☐ NO *(If "YES" indicate country or area)*

17. TYPING ABILITY ☐ YES ☐ NO WPM_____	18. WHEN SERVING OVERSEAS WILL YOUR DEPENDENTS ACCOMPANY YOU? ☐ YES ☐ NO	19. BIRTHPLACE OF SPOUSE US CITIZEN: ☐ YES ☐ NO

20. DEPENDENT DATA			21. INDICATE CONTEMPLATED DATE AND PLACE OF RETIREMENT
NAME	RELATIONSHIP	DATE OF BIRTH	

22. CURRENT ADDRESS OF DEPENDENTS	23. DEPENDENTS PROJECTED LOCATION WHEN YOU ARE ASSIGNED TO A SHORT TOUR AREA	24. LEAVE MAILING ADDRESS FOR CONTACT PURPOSES
☐ OWN ☐ RENT ☐ GOVT QTRS		PHONE (____) ____ A/C

DA FORM 1 MAR 76 **2635**   REPLACES EDITION OF 1 JUL 67. WHICH IS OBSOLETE.

Enlisted Preference Statement
(sample)

An application for deletion or curtailment of an overseas assignment can be made while the soldier is on emergency leave, if he has been granted that leave to return to CONUS due to extreme family problems. If, once the soldier arrives in CONUS, he discovers that the problem can be resolved only by remaining in CONUS, the soldier should then go to the nearest Army installation or activity that has a personnel or administrative office and request the reassignment through that office. If it is not possible to go to an Army installation, the soldier should telephone Headquarters, Department of the Army (HQDA DAPC-EPA-C) during duty hours. As of January 1986, that number was (202) 325-7730. HQDA can then advise the soldier of further action he may need to take.

EXCHANGING ASSIGNMENTS

Commonly called "swapping," exchanging assignments is one way you can control where you will live and work. The process is simple in principal, but it is not always so simple to implement.

Two soldiers in differing locations must agree on a personal basis to exchange assignments. Both must be the same pay grade and be serving in the same MOS, with similar qualifications. In addition, all commanders involved must agree to the swap. Requests for an assignment exchange cannot be made directly to the commander at the location where the soldier would like to be assigned. Each soldier must work out the arrangements on a person-to-person basis with another soldier wanting to be assigned to the present location of the first. Official correspondence and government mailing cannot be used in making arrangements for an assignment exchange.

Once arrangements have been made, one of the soldiers must submit a request to his installation commander. That commander then coordinates the action, if it is approved, with the installation commander of the second soldier. The exchange will be disapproved if one of the soldiers has received assignment instructions.

The soldiers must pay all expenses incurred for this relocation. The Army will not move the families of soldiers exchanging assignments. Further, any travel time needed is counted as ordinary leave.

An excellent source of information on possible stateside swaps can be found in the weekly issues of *Army Times*. In a "want-ad" format, *Army Times* lists soldiers by MOS, rank, name and address—and includes those areas in which the particular soldier would be interested. If another soldier is interested in the location/assignment of the individual listed in the ad, all contact information is readily available. *Army Times* also provides a map so that each soldier can determine exactly where the new installation is located.

ASSIGNMENT OF MARRIED COUPLES

Special consideration can be afforded to married Army couples, defined as those couples in which both individuals are members of the Army. Specifically, the Army has established a voluntary Army couples program, which provides consideration for joint assignments. Such joint assignments, of course, must be consistent with the needs of the Army. The Army's goal for the Married Army Couples (MAC) Program is that 90 percent of the soldiers enrolled in the program will automatically receive joint assignments. Soldiers married to members of other branches of the military are not eligible for the MAC Program, nor are soldiers married to civilians.

Once a couple has enrolled in the program, consideration for joint assignment is continuous and computerized. Whenever one member is under consideration for a PCS, the spouse is also considered for assignment to the same installation, command, or general area. While consideration is automatic, assignment is not. An Army spouse cannot be assigned if he does not meet all necessary qualifications, and is not in an MOS and grade where a valid Army requirement exists at the proposed assignment. The needs of the Army must still be of primary consideration in any reassignment. Married Army couples are still required to fulfill their military obligations regardless of their own assignment location or that of their spouse.

Joint overseas assignments are sometimes harder to obtain. There are several reasons for this. First, the overseas major command must give its permission for the joint assignment. If the couple has minor dependents, such permission is more difficult to obtain for isolated tours where facilities are not available for dependent care. The danger of the Demilitarized Zone in Korea can mean that permission for joint assignment there is more difficult to obtain, as well. Joint assignments to Germany are usually possible because of the large number of authorized slots in a wide variety of MOSs. Hawaii is almost impossible for a joint assignment because so many slots are reserved there through guaranteed assignments for reenlisting and recruiting efforts.

Whenever possible, married Army couples can receive concurrent overseas assignments, if they so desire. Ideally, they would be assigned to the same overseas command, or at least to the same general location. If such assignments are not possible, MILPERCEN will still give consideration to a request that each spouse serve a short-term tour in differing locations but at the same time. In this manner, joint assignments after the short tour are facilitated.

If the Army spouse of a soldier is assigned to an overseas tour, but arrives at a later date than that of the first, the soldier with the earliest Date Eligible for Return from Overseas (DEROS) may normally extend his tour to coincide with the later DEROS of the spouse. The spouse who arrives last determines when the Army couple returns to CONUS.

Problems can be avoided in the MAC Program if couples follow a few basic rules. First, they should enroll in the MAC Program as soon as possible. Once one servicemember has received orders, it is too late for the couple to enroll. They may, however, initiate a request for joint domicile, which can be handled through MILPERCEN on a manual, versus computerized, basis. In fact, the old Joint Domicile Program (prior to October 1985) was based entirely on individual requests for joint assignments, handled manually on a case-by-case basis.

For newly married Army couples, it is recommended that they join the MAC Program within the first 60 days after they are married.

To enroll in the MAC Program, one of the soldiers must fill out a DA Form 4187 through his MILPO. After the MILPO clerk verifies the marriage, one SIDPERS transaction is completed, listing names and social security numbers of both spouses, in addition to their current assignments. One transaction updates the master files for both soldiers. Under the following circumstances, both soldiers must fill out DA Form 4187 and two transactions must be made.

- If the Army couple has married, but they carry different surnames. (Usually this occurs when the wife elects to retain her maiden name.)
- If the Army couple consists of one officer and one enlisted soldier. (Since assignments for officers and for enlisted soldiers are handled through different offices, two transactions are required.)

The soldiers involved should inform the MILPO clerk of the necessity of filing two transactions under these circumstances.

Divorces can also cause problems for the MAC Program. Unless one of the divorced soldiers completes paperwork to remove the couple's names from the MAC Program, they will continue to receive joint assignments.

The MAC Program functions only for computer-generated assignments. If one soldier reenlists for a guaranteed assignment, his spouse will not receive a joint assignment under the MAC Program. Initiating a joint domicile request is the couple's only alternative. Even joint domicile requests cannot be honored, however, if one soldier from the couple arranges an exchange of assignments with another soldier. The reason? The military bears none of the costs associated with assignment exchanges. On the other hand, if MILPERCEN were to approve a joint domicile request, the PCS would be a government-paid move.

OVERSEAS ASSIGNMENTS

Overseas assignments are an integral part of the military lifestyle. If you have adequate information and preparation, such tours can be very satisfying and can prove to be the highlight of your career. Clearly, some overseas assignments are more desirable than others, but Army regulations (AR 614-30) emphasize the need for "equitable distribution of overseas assignments, considering both desirable and undesirable locations."

Which assignments are "desirable" is a debatable subject. One soldier may consider a particular location he has served to be ideal, a true paradise. Another may consider the same location to be nearly intolerable. The best advice you can follow is to gather factual information but reserve judgment. Keeping a positive attitude before and after arriving "in country" can be instrumental in making your first overseas tour an enjoyable experience.

The Army has several programs to make the move overseas more amenable, but perhaps the most valuable is the sponsorship program. Once a servicemember has orders, he should be contacted shortly by an assigned sponsor from the gaining unit. If no contact is initiated by the overseas unit, the soldier should write to the First Sergeant of the upcoming assignment and request a sponsor. Sponsors provide the individual with information about the unit, civilian economy, housing, educational facilities, and other information to make the move more comfortable.

A second important program is the Overseas Orientation Program, a normal part of the out-processing procedure. All personnel on overseas assignment orders are required to attend the orientation. Family members are encouraged to attend as well, whether or not they will be accompanying the servicemember overseas. Three films are normally a part of this orientation: "Going Our Way," which presents information of the actual travel; "Personal Affairs," which covers topics such as wills, insurance, powers of attorney, records, and files; and "Travel Entitlements," which introduces the soldier to the various entitlements and encourages him to seek guidance on specific details of the entitlements.

While the Army will decide where you will be assigned, you have an impact on how long the tour will be. Basically, accompanied tours (when family members accompany the servicemember) are longer than unaccompanied tours. Length of tour varies with location and dependents status. In addition, the soldier who has no dependents and is in his first three-year enlistment often can serve a shorter tour. In the accompanying chart, the first two columns refer to servicemembers who have dependents and choose the accompanied or unaccompanied tour; the third column refers to personnel who have no dependents, and who have reenlisted at least once or whose first enlistment was a four-, five-, or six-year enlistment; and the fourth column refers to soldiers who have no dependents and who are still in their first three-year enlistment.

Length of Overseas Tour

Country	With Dependents	Without Dependents	Careerist No Dependents	First-termer No Dependents
Alaska				
Anchorage,				
Elemendorf, AFB,				
Ft. Richardson,				
Fairbanks area,				
Ft. Wainwright	36	24	36	24
Ft. Greely	24	12	12	12
Argentina	36	24	36	24
Australia	36	24	36	24
Austria	36	24*	36	18
Bahrain Island	24	12	12	12
Barbados	36	18	36	18
Belgium	36	24*	36	18
Belize	24	12	12	12
Bolivia	24	18	18	18
Brazil	36	24	36	24
Canada	36	24	36	24
Chile	36	24	36	24
Colombia	36	24	36	24
Costa Rica	36	24	36	24
Denmark	36	24*	36	18
Dominican Republic	36**	24	36	24
Ecuador	36	18	36	18
Egypt				
Sinai	—	12	12	12
All other locations	24	18	18	18

Country	With Dependents	Without Dependents	Careerist No Dependents	First-termer No Dependents
El Salvador				
San Salvador	24	24	24	24
All other locations	—	12	12	12
France	36	24*	36	18
Germany	36	24*	36	18
Greece				
Athens, Elevsis, Katsimidhi, Korpi, Piraeus	30	18	18	18
Crete, Iraklion	24	18	18	18
Namfi	24	12	12	12
Thessaloniki	24	15	15	15
All other locations	—	12	12	12
Guam	24	15	15	15
Guatemala	36	24	36	24
Hawaii				
Kauai, KMC Kilauea	30	18	18	18
Pohakuloa training area	24	18	18	18
All other locations	36	24	36	24
Honduras	24	18	18	18
Iceland	24	12	12	12
India	24	12	12	12
Indonesia	24	12	12	12
Israel	24	12	12	12
Italy				
Naz Sciaves	—	15	15	15
Mt. Finale Ligure	—	12	12	12
San Vito	30	18	18	18
Sigonella, Sicily	36	24	24	24
All other locations	36	24*	36	18
Jamaica	24	12	12	12
Japan/Okinawa				
Akizuki Kure	—***	12	12	12
Misawa	30	18	18	18
All other locations	36	24*	36	18
Johnston Island	—	12	12	12
Jordan	24	12	12	12
Kenya	24	18	18	18

Country	With Dependents	Without Dependents	Careerist No Dependents	First-termer No Dependents
Korea	24	12	12	12
Kuwait	24	12	12	12
Lebanon	—	12	12	12
Liberia	24	12	12	12
Luxembourg	36	24*	36	18
Morocco	24	15	15	15
Malaysia	24	24	24	24
Netherlands	36	24*	36	18
Nicaragua	24	18	18	18
Norway	36	24*	36	18
Okinawa *(See Japan)*				
Oman	24	12	12	12
Pakistan	24	18	18	18
Panama				
Galeta Island	24	18	18	18
All other locations	36	24	36	24
Paraguay	24	18	18	18
Peru	30	18	18	18
Philippines				
Camp John Hay	36	18	36	18
Clark Air Base, Manila	36	24	36	24
Portugal				
Azores	24	15	15	15
All other locations	36	24	36	24
Puerto Rico	36	15	15	15
Saudi Arabia	24	12	12	12
Somalia	24	12	12	12
Spain	36	24*	36	18
Sudan	24	12	12	12
Thailand	24	12	12	12
Tunisia	24	12	12	12
Turkey				
Ankara, Izmir	24	15	15	15
All other locations	—	12	12	12
United Arab Emirates	24	12	12	12
United Kingdom	36	24*	36	18
Uruguay	36	24	36	24

Country	With Dependents	Without Dependents	Careerist No Dependents	First-termer No Dependents
Venezuela	24	18	18	18
Virgin Islands	36	24	36	24

* Soldiers serving an unaccompanied tour and who are in their first three-year enlistment have an 18-month tour, the same as the first-term soldier with no dependents.

** Regardless of status, all personnel assigned to the U.S. Army Facilities Engineering Support Agency with duty in Santo Domingo must serve a 24-month tour, whether accompanied or unaccompanied.

*** Once servicemembers have arrived in Akizuki Kure and have been able to observe living conditions personally, the commander may approve a 24-month accompanied tour for the soldier on an individual basis.

The Soldier with Dependents

All soldiers with dependents who would be unable to care for themselves in the absence of the servicemember must file a Family Care Plan with their unit commander. Personnel in grades E1 through E6 must have the plan approved. In addition, all personnel with less then three years of military service must receive counseling with regard to their dual responsibilities to the Army and to their families. Examples of soldiers who would need to file the Family Care Plan are single soldiers or soldiers with an in-service spouse, with minor or handicapped dependents. The military requires such a plan so that the soldier will be prepared in the event that he is assigned to an overseas location where dependents may not live.

As the "Length of Overseas Tour" chart indicates, soldiers with dependents have a choice in many instances as to whether they will take their dependents overseas. If the soldier chooses an accompanied tour, but has insufficient time remaining on the current enlistment to serve the entire length of the accompanied tour, he is required to extend or reenlist prior to the actual move.

The question arises when the soldier is not sure whether it is best to choose the accompanied or unaccompanied tour. If undecided, the servicemember can possibly retain some options by selecting the accompanied tour and then going overseas originally unaccompanied. If, after arriving at the new assignment and assessing the situation, the individual decides it is better for his family *not* to make the move, he can request a change in tour from accompanied to unaccompanied. Although the overseas commander is authorized to approve such a request, the request must be made within six months for shorter tours and twelve months for longer tours.

The opposite scenario is not quite so easy. If the soldier originally selects an unaccompanied tour and later decides it is more advantageous to have the tour accompanied, he may have difficulty making that change. Family members can join the soldier overseas, traveling at their own expense, and then the soldier may request command sponsorship. The soldier must have enough time remaining on the current enlistment, however, to serve the accompanied tour length, or have 12 months of remaining service *after* the family arrives—whichever is *longer.* Once the family members have been approved as command-sponsored, their travel expenses will be paid by the government for their *return trip* back to the United States.

In some overseas areas no accompanied tours are allowed. Servicemembers sometimes decide to bring the family along at personal expense in a noncommand-sponsored status. Such a decision can have serious consequences. First, no government housing will be available. Use of the commissary and post exchange will also not be allowed for noncommand-sponsored individuals. Dependents will not be authorized to use Department of Defense dependent schools. In the event of a need for evacuation of family members, the evacuation program will not be specifically structured to support noncommand-sponsored family members. These are all factors that must be weighed carefully before deciding to take the family.

When an unaccompanied tour is the first selection, the service family is entitled to a government-paid move, including transportation of dependents and household goods, to another location of their choice within the continental United States. Government-paid moves to Alaska or Hawaii, to Puerto Rico, or to other U.S. territories or possessions are sometimes possible.

While the decision whether to take family members overseas is never an easy one, the soldier can receive counseling on this decision through several sources. The Army Community Service can advise the family on financial matters and how an accompanied tour may affect their financial situation. The legal office can provide advice on any legal matters that may be more complicated when the servicemember is overseas. Counseling of a more general nature can be obtained through the Army chaplain or the unit's First Sergeant.

Marital status sometimes changes while the servicemember is overseas. Such changes can affect the length of tour. If military members acquire dependents (i.e., through marriage) and request command sponsorship for the new dependents, the overseas commander may approve sponsorship only if the servicemember has sufficient time remaining on his enlistment to serve an accompanied tour. Newly acquired family members with command sponsorship can travel to the United States at government expense. On the other hand, if a servicemember is divorced and does not retain physical custody or financial responsibility for dependents, he will be considered to have no dependents, and the tour length will be appropriately adjusted. Similar adjustments to tour length can be made when two married servicemembers have joint domicile overseas and one spouse separates from service and becomes a dependent.

When a servicemember's spouse is also in the military, the couple may request joint domicile when one or the other receives voluntary or involuntary assignment overseas. Both must have served a minimum of 12 months, however, at their current duty stations in order for the request to be approved. In addition, both must individually meet the normal requirements for the overseas assignment. A vacancy must exist for soldiers in their respective skill areas. Approved joint domicile means that soldiers will be assured of assignment within 50 miles of each other, or within one hour's driving time.

Accompanied tours do not mean that the family can necessarily travel with the servicemember who is headed overseas. Family travel status is based on the projected availability of housing, either government quarters or local economy housing. Three possibilities exist: concurrent travel, deferred travel, or disapproved travel.

Concurrent travel means the family travels with the service member. It is based on a projected availability of housing within 60 days after the family's arrival. If the projected availability is between 61 and 140 days, the family's travel will be deferred until housing is available. Families in government quarters at the current assignment will be allowed to retain those quarters for up to 140 days if deferred travel is approved. Families living off-post may either stay at the current location with no movement of household goods or move to a temporary location, provided the household goods are separated into those awaiting shipment overseas and those being placed in storage.

When the projected availability of overseas housing is greater than 140 days, family travel will be disapproved. This does not mean that the family cannot join the servicemember at a later date. Once the servicemember arrives at his new assignment and locates adequate housing for the dependents, he may request family travel. If housing does not become available, the servicemember may request that the length of tour be adjusted to an unaccompanied tour.

Concurrent travel for family members can be based on the availability of temporary housing with a friend or relative in the overseas area, provided the friend or relative is not occupying government quarters. From the individuals providing the temporary housing, the soldier must secure a statement that his family can share accommodations with friends or relatives until they are able to find housing for themselves. He then forwards this statement, with his own request for concurrent family travel, to the overseas commander. In addition, the soldier should indicate the availability of such quarters when completing the reassignment processing.

One other method of ensuring concurrent travel exists. If the soldier's family has been denied concurrent travel based on the projected availability of housing, the soldier's sponsor may be able to locate housing on the civilian economy for the incoming family. This is not, however, an easy task to accomplish.

First, the sponsor and the new soldier rarely are personally acquainted, and their choices in housing may vary greatly. Second, the sponsor has no obligation to undertake such a search and may not agree to do so. The soldier would have to request assistance from the sponsor, provide the sponsor with the necessary power of attorney to sign the rental or lease contract for the stateside soldier, and, of course, provide any moneys required to complete the arrangements. In addition, the housing located by the sponsor would have to be approved as adequate by the Housing Referral Office overseas. Once this approval was obtained, the family members could be granted concurrent travel.

Soldiers in grades E1 through E4 are now authorized increased family travel benefits. Previously, junior enlisted personnel with less than two years of service were not authorized travel for family members at government expense and were limited to 225 pounds of unaccompanied baggage. Now, however, family members can be authorized government-paid travel and up to 1,500 pounds of personal property for shipment overseas. This total weight limit includes unaccompanied baggage, unaccompanied goods, and household goods.

These changes did not affect housing policies, however. Junior enlisted personnel with less than two years of service cannot obtain government quarters. They must live on the civilian economy. One possibility for soldiers in grade E4 nearing their two years of service (within 120 days) is to request a temporary deferment in the overseas assignment so that the servicemember will have completed two years of service before the PCS date. If deferment is granted, the soldier and his family will be authorized to use government quarters overseas if available and to ship 7,000 pounds of personal property (at government expense) instead of 1,500 pounds.

In addition, junior enlisted personnel are authorized to ship a privately owned vehicle (POV)—a car, truck, or motorcycle—if POV-shipment is authorized for that particular country or area.

The Soldier with No Dependents

Soldiers with no dependents follow many of the same general guidelines as soldiers with dependents. The length of their overseas tour depends on whether they have obtained career status. Basically, soldiers in their first three-year enlistment are not considered to have career status and can therefore serve a shorter overseas tour in many cases, as indicated previously on the chart of tour lengths.

The information in the remainder of this chapter applies to all soldiers, whether or not they have dependents.

Pregnant Servicewomen

How pregnancy affects overseas tours for servicewomen depends on when the soldier finds out she is pregnant. Generally, a servicewoman scheduled for a PCS to an overseas assignment becomes ineligible for the move once she finds out she is pregnant. Exceptions to this policy can be granted through Headquarters, Department of the Army, at HQDA (DAPC-EPA-C), Alexandria, VA 22331. If joint domicile has already been approved and if the soldier can obtain a clearance for overseas travel from military medical authorities, a local commander (06 or higher) can approve the request. Under no circumstance, however, will a pregnant servicemember be allowed to travel overseas after the seventh month of pregnancy.

When a soldier becomes pregnant while overseas, her tour sometimes must be curtailed. For instance, if a noncombatant evacuation is ordered, pregnant servicewomen who have reached the seventh month of pregnancy will have their tours curtailed and will be evacuated. The tours of soldiers in earlier stages of pregnancy may be curtailed on an individual basis. Such curtailments are based on the ability of the soldier to perform her duties, medical availability of both prenatal and postnatal care, proximity to hostilities, and danger to the welfare of the unborn child (e.g., inadequate resources such as housing, child care, or infant food).

In addition, if the soldier would be required to involuntarily extend her tour for more than 90 days on a long tour or for more than 60 days on a short tour, based on travel restrictions and her expected delivery date, her tour will be curtailed and she will be returned to the United States. However, six weeks after the birth of her child and subsequent release from in-patient status, the servicewoman may be reassigned overseas if she had not completed a sufficient amount of her tour to be credited with a completed tour.

The bar to assignment overseas based on failure to meet weight requirements does apply to pregnant soldiers. This means that a servicemember whose tour was curtailed because of pregnancy cannot return overseas unless her weight is within Army standards six weeks after the birth of her child. It also applies to soldiers requesting exceptions based on joint domicile or for other reasons. If the pregnant soldier is not within Army weight standards, the exception must be disapproved.

Deferments, Deletions, and Curtailments

Quite logically the Army desires to keep deferments, deletions, and curtailments of overseas assignments to a minimum. All can tend to affect personnel readiness adversely. A number of reasons—mostly compassionate—exist, however, for each of these cases.

Deferments are temporary delays in the PCS date, usually for less than 90 days. Except for emergency situations, deferments must be requested within 30 days of receiving assignment instructions. If the assignment instructions are for a light infantry division, the request for deferment must be submitted within 15 days after receiving instructions.

Deletions are longer delays. When a deletion is approved, the soldier normally will be stabilized at the present assignment for up to one year or until the problem—under which the deletion was approved,—has been resolved.

The following conditions are given as examples of reasons for deferments or deletions. There are a number of other such conditions.

Deferments of not more than 90 days may be granted when a family member other than a spouse or child dies within 90 days of the scheduled overseas movement date. Deletions are usually approved when the servicemember's spouse or child dies after the servicemember receives assignment instructions.

When a family member requires hospitalization of less than 90 days, deferments can be granted. In the more severe case where hospitalization is expected to extend beyond 90 days, a deletion can be approved. Terminal illness of a family member, where death is expected within a year, is another reason for deletion. A domestic hardship, in which the presence of the soldier can result in a permanent solution, can be a valid reason to request a deferment, as can a scheduled court date or a pending child custody resolution in divorce, legal separation, or a desertion case. Documented cases of child abuse or rape of the servicemember's spouse or child can be the basis for deletions when the presence of the servicemember is essential to resolve associate problems.

As mentioned previously, pregnancy of the servicemember is a cause for deletion; pregnancy of a spouse, however, is not a cause. Deferments may be granted when the spouse is at least in the eighth month of pregnancy as of the date the soldier is scheduled to report to an overseas assignment.

Training is another valid reason for either deferment or deletion from an overseas assignment. If, after selection for Basic or Advanced Noncommissioned Officer Education System (NCOES) attendance, a soldier receives overseas assignment instruction, the assignment can be deferred for up to 90 days to allow the servicemember to attend or complete training. The assignment can be deleted for more than 90 days for the same cause or for preselection to attend Officer Candidate School (OCS).

Other situations that may be traumatic to the servicemember are not, in and of themselves, considered valid conditions for deferments. Among these situations are divorce, legal separation, family members' allergies that would be aggravated in the overseas climate, financial problems, or problems associated with home ownership.

Once the soldier is overseas, his tour can be curtailed (or cut short) based on some of the same types of reasons approved for deferment or deletion. The death of an immediate family member can be cause for curtailment, as can urgent health problems of a family member living with the soldier overseas. Health problems that necessitate the return of family members to the United States are not, however, necessarily causes for curtailment of the soldier's overseas tour. When family members must return from overseas before the servicemember, the soldier may request an adjusted length of tour based on his unaccompanied status. A pregnant soldier may have her tour curtailed, as detailed previously.

Volunteering

While the Army may assign you to an overseas tour involuntarily, you may also volunteer for such tours. Once the request for an overseas assignment is approved, volunteers are given top priority for overseas assignments, either for long or for short tours.

Approval is based on the vacancies existing at the overseas location and on the requirement that the volunteer has completed a minimum of 12 months at his current station (if the current station is beyond the initial training assignments). In addition, the volunteer must have completed initial entry training (basic training and advanced individual training or on-the-job training) before going overseas. Soldiers are not qualified for overseas assignments if they are overweight, awaiting trial or the results of trial by Special or General Court Martial, under investigation for criminal or subversive activities, or being processed for involuntary separation from service.

Once overseas, the soldier may also volunteer for extension of his tour and for intertheater and intratheater transfers. (Involuntary extensions and transfers are sometimes necessary as well.) If the voluntary extension is approved and the soldier subsequently requests a cancellation of the extension, that request could be disapproved by the overseas commander. If the servicemember has already begun serving the extension, a request for cancellation of the extension cannot be approved.

Regulations governing requests for extension are detailed. For most long tours, the request must be approved no later than 12 months before the scheduled DEROS. Junior enlisted personnel (E1 through E4) can shorten that period to 6 months before DEROS if assigned to a long tour in Europe, unless that assignment is with the Allied Command Europe, in which case the 12-month deadline holds. If language training is required for the Allied Command Europe position, the 12-month deadline is expanded for all soldiers to a period of 12 months *plus* the length of language training desired. Time periods change for short-tour extensions to 6 months before DEROS, and then only if reassignment instructions have not already been received. Short tours in Korea and Ft. Greely, Alaska, have even shorter deadlines—4 months before DEROS, and again, only if reassignment instructions have not already been received.

Normally any length of extension between 6 and 18 months can be approved for each extension request. Extensions for Allied Command Europe can be between 6 and 12 months, however. Shorter extensions can be approved by the overseas commander for the servicemember whose dependents, living at the overseas assignment, are restricted from travel because of advanced pregnancy of the wife, recent birth of a child, or serious illness of a dependent.

Voluntary extensions expand the time that a soldier spends at a single location. Also possible are voluntary intertheater and intratheater transfers, which extend the overseas time but at a new location. An intertheater transfer is an overseas transfer from one theater to another; an intratheater transfer is from one location within a given theater to another location within the same theater.

Overseas theaters are geographic areas, as follows: Africa and Middle East Asia area (AMEA); European area (EURA); Far East and Pacific area (FEPA); and South American and Caribbean area (SACA).

For intertheater transfers, the soldier must complete the current overseas tour he is serving before being reassigned, but the request for voluntary transfer should be submitted no later than 5 months before DEROS for short tours and no later than 10 months before DEROS for long tours. Requests are submitted on DA Form 2635 (Enlisted Preference Statement). A complete tour will also be served at the new assignment.

For voluntary intratheater transfers, the soldier must serve a complete tour at the new assignment but does not necessarily have to complete the tour at the current assignment before being transferred. All voluntary transfers must be to a valid vacancy and must not necessitate two PCS moves within one fiscal year.

Extending a long tour through the Overseas Extension Incentive Program can mean extra money or benefits. If your MOS is designated by MILPERCEN as a space-imbalanced (or shortage) MOS, or if the normal turnaround time between the States and overseas assignments is less than 24 months for your MOS, you are eligible for the program. Extending adds $80 a month to your salary or it provides you with either 30 days nonchargeable leave, or 15 days nonchargeable leave and space-required travel to and from the States. See your local MILPO office for the most current list of qualifying MOSs.

Homebase and Advance Assignment Program

Servicemembers in grades E5 and above are eligible to participate in the Homebase and Advance Assignment Program (HAAP). Under HAAP a soldier's current stateside assignment is considered his homebase. When the individual receives an overseas assignment to a 12-month short-tour dependent-restricted area, he is returned to the homebase assignment area, after the overseas assignment, when at all possible. If a return to the homebase is not possible, the soldier is at least informed of the assignment that will follow the overseas short tour *before* leaving overseas location.

Soldiers assigned to 18-month unaccompanied tours overseas may participate in the homebase portion of HAAP if they are in grade E5 or above and if reassignment to the homebase is possible. The advanced assignment portion of HAAP is not available to them, however.

Voluntary extensions by the soldier will automatically cancel any prearranged HAAP assignment.

Important Details for an Overseas PCS

Numerous details are involved with any PCS, but those details are magnified in importance with an overseas move. Getting an overseas sponsor through the new unit will be immensely helpful. Equally important are attending the orientation program and having dependents attend.

Passports are not required for military personnel in most cases. Passports are necessary, however, if soldiers wish to travel on leave in the overseas area. Dependents must have passports to accompany the servicemember. Each military installation stateside has a passport office that can assist the soldier in obtaining the necessary forms. Since the passport process is not speedy, requesting passports as soon as possible is advisable.

The soldier must keep a number of documents in his immediate possession at all times while traveling to an overseas assignment. Among them are the military identification (ID) card, two ID tags (dog tags), a copy of reassignment orders, a Request and Authorization for Leave (if appropriate), an official passport (if required), military records packet, a shot record (PHS Form 731), and the Travelope and/or airline ticket. In addition, the basic issue of military clothing and uniforms must be with the soldier, as well as inserts for the protective field mask if vision so necessitates.

The Travelope (DA Form 4600) gives important information on travel and port of call. Soldiers should pick up their Travelope (and airline ticket if appropriate) at least four days prior to the scheduled port of call date. If the soldier is taking leave before going overseas, he should get the Travelope before leaving the stateside installation.

While traveling overseas, the only medications that a servicemember or dependents can carry are prescribed medications. Further, all such medications must be properly recorded in the individual health records. (Health records are to be in the possession of the individual carrying the medication.) Keeping medicines in their proper pharmaceutical containers is also important.

Emergencies En Route to an Overseas Assignment

Medical Care

Medical emergencies that arise for either the servicemember or accompanying dependents should be handled through military hospitals, if at all possible, when the individuals are en route to a new assignment. Military hospitals include all branches of the military as well as the U.S. Coast Guard facilities. Most maps clearly mark military facilities. If the servicemember is hospitalized, it is critical that proper authorities be notified. The treatment facility should contact both the Red Cross and the soldier's Military Personnel Center Personnel Assistance Point (PAP). The PAP should be listed on the Travelope, DA Form 4600. These authorities should be notified on the soldier's location, the nature of the illness or injury, and the anticipated length of hospitalization. The PAP can advise the soldier on what actions to take on release from the treatment facility.

If no military hospital is nearby and the illness or injury is an emergency, the servicemember should seek medical attention from civilian sources. If the treatment is not an emergency, but is elective in nature, the cost of treatment will usually not be reimbursed by the government. The same rules apply for dependents of the servicemember. If the soldier must pay for emergency medical treatment, he should get a detailed bill showing diagnosis, treatment, costs, and whether the treatment was routine or emergency in nature. A claim for reimbursement of medical costs should then be submitted to military officials as soon as possible.

Medical emergencies could arise when the soldier (and dependents) have already left the United States but have not yet arrived at the new assignment location. If in a foreign country and no U.S. military medical facilities are available, the soldier should contact the nearest U.S. embassy or American consulate for advice.

(One comforting note is that nongovernment friends and relatives visiting a soldier overseas can be treated for medical conditions at military facilities, on a reimbursable basis.)

Financial Crisis

En route to an overseas assignment, soldiers who find themselves without funds for transportation to their port of call should first contact the Finance and Accounting Office at the nearest military installation. With proper military ID, reassignment orders, and individual pay records (from the records packet), the soldier may be able to receive casual pay. Such pay would later be deducted from standard end-of-month pay.

If casual pay cannot be arranged, the soldier's next sources of help are (in order) the American Red Cross, the nearest Army Community Service where referral can be made to the Army Emergency Relief Office, and the nearest military transportation office, on a military post or base.

Once overseas, the soldier in financial crisis should contact the nearest U.S. military installation for help, or the U.S. embassy or American consulate if no military installations are located within that country.

Lost Airline Ticket

Losing a ticket can certainly become a financial crisis. The first step a soldier should take to resolve this particular problem is to contact the commercial carrier on which the ticket was to be used and request a replacement ticket. If this cannot be arranged, the Travelers Aid Office located in many major terminals may be able to help. Travelers Aid specifically serves military travelers. The final step is to contact the PAP, calling either collect or Autovon, if available, and requesting aid and instructions. If the soldier is already in a foreign country when he loses the ticket, U.S. military installations, the U.S. embassy, or the American consulate's office are the sources of aid available.

Family Crisis

Serious illness or death of an immediate family member can create the need for an emergency leave request. Immediate family members include mother, father, spouse, child, brother, or sister. The request should be made directly to the assigned PAP by calling collect or Autovon, if available. In addition, contacting the American Red Cross, so that they can verify the emergency, can aid the soldier in expediting the request for emergency leave. The local Red Cross should contact the soldier's PAP after verification.

Lost or Stolen Documents

A missing ID card should be reported to military police at the nearest military installation, as well as to the local police in the area where the card was lost or stolen. The Post Adjutant General's Office at the nearest military post may be able to issue a new ID card if the soldier can provide copies of military personnel records and reassignment orders. In each case, however, the servicemember should report the problem to the PAP as well.

Lost military pay records can result in a delay in receiving military pay. The PAP is again the primary authority that needs to be notified. A loan can possibly be arranged through the AER once the soldier arrives at the new duty station. Lost shot records, health records, or dental records should also be reported to the PAP. If the losses occur after the soldier has left the United States, the new unit commander is the primary individual to be notified.

Lost Baggage

Commercial carriers can frequently lose baggage. When the soldier is en route overseas, such a loss can prove to be extremely inconvenient. This inconvenience is magnified if important documents were left in checked baggage. Therefore, it is critical that documents remain in the possession of the servicemember, in carryon luggage. Recovering lost baggage can be expedited if a copy of reassignment orders is placed in each piece of luggage before the trip begins. Another suggestion that may decrease the chance of lost luggage is to reclaim and recheck baggage at each point in the journey where a change in carriers is required. The soldier then can assume greater control over his possessions.

The Soldier's Role Overseas

The primary role of the overseas soldier is the same as that of his stateside counterpart—to fulfill mission requirements. Overseas assignments, however, carry additional roles that should not be overlooked.

Foreign nationals get their principal opinions of America through the Americans they see. American allies build good or bad impressions of "true Americans" by viewing soldiers and dependents living overseas. These Americans become unofficial ambassadors. It is not a job they may choose to decline; it is forced upon them by their very location in the foreign country. Poor conduct by the soldier can result in his being returned to the United States under punitive action; poor conduct on the part of dependents can result in the overseas commander requiring the early involuntary return of dependents to the United States.

The role of ambassador can be complicated by the differing customs and lifestyles in overseas communities. By accepting and adjusting to different social concepts and beliefs, the soldier can gain the respect of the host countrymen. A positive attitude toward differing customs goes a long way toward making adjustment easier. It might be helpful for the soldier to recall that his customs seem as strange to the foreign nationals as their customs seem to him. Further, their pride in their heritage is every bit as strong as the soldier's pride in American history.

An overseas assignment is similar to a stateside assignment in one respect: it will be only as rewarding as the soldier makes it.

6

Looking Sharp

The old axiom, You can't tell a book by its cover, may hold for many circumstances in life, but the military person is frequently judged by his appearance. The military presence of a soldier, his professionalism as a soldier, the self-discipline and pride the soldier possesses, and the esprit de corps of the individual are all reflected in daily grooming habits and appearance.

The Army places great emphasis on a well-groomed, neat appearance, which influences the opinions of both superiors and peers, as well. Commanders and NCOs, who have significant impact on the promotions of their soldiers, are tasked by the Army to ensure that military personnel under their command maintain a neat and soldierly appearance. Regulations remind them that "A vital ingredient of the Army's strength and military effectiveness is the pride and self-discipline that American soldiers bring to their Service" (AR 670-1). The soldier's appearance becomes a reflection of that pride. In that light, it becomes the military duty of the soldier to maintain a soldierly appearance at all times—an appearance greatly affected by physical fitness, weight control, and care for uniform standards. (See chapter 2 for information on physical fitness and weight control.)

CHARGE!

Through AR 600-20, Chapter 5, the Army recognizes certain exceptions to the standard uniform wear based on religious practices and beliefs. Any granted exceptions can be temporarily revoked at the discretion of the commander because of health or safety requirements, or if mission requirements so dictate. The exceptions for religious practices consist of allowing:

- Visible religious articles and jewelry that comply with authorized nonreligious articles and jewelry.
- Religious articles and jewelry that are not visible or apparent when the soldier is in uniform.
- Religious skullcaps of plain design and standard color, provided they do not exceed six inches in diameter. Wearing of skullcaps is restricted to living quarters, indoor dining facilities, and worship service locations.

Soldiers desiring other types of deviations from standard military uniform appearance must request exceptions from HQDA, following guidelines provided in AR 600-20, Chapter 5. Once approval from HQDA has been received, the local commander can approve the exception, retaining the right to revoke the exception temporarily based on health, safety, or mission requirements.

Since conforming to military standards can enhance your image in the eyes of your commander, it behooves you to pay close attention to what the Army expects in appearance.

GROOMING

Haircuts

The basic premise of the Army standard for haircuts is that the hair be neat, clean, and of an appropriate length and style so that it does not interfere with the proper wearing of headgear or protective masks. Dyes, tints, and bleaches are permissible, provided the resulting color occurs naturally in human hair. Faddish or extreme hairstyles are considered inappropriate for the soldier, as are hairstyles that appear ragged or unkempt.

The male soldier must wear a style with a tapered appearance. While blockcut fullness in the back is permitted in moderation, the overall look must project a tapered effect. The length of the hair must be such that, when combed, it neither falls over the ears or eyebrows nor touches the collar. Closely cut hair at the back of the neck can touch the collar, but the length of the hair cannot.

The female soldier must also choose a style with a neat appearance, not excessive or extreme. Her hair may not fall over her eyebrows either, but it may touch the collar at the back of the neck, provided it does not extend below the collar. Hairnets are not authorized unless required for health or safety reasons. (In such cases, hairnets will be provided free of cost.) Any barrettes, clips, or pins used in the hair must be transparent or the same color as the soldier's hair. In addition, such hair-holding devices must be placed inconspicuously in the hairstyle. No hair ornaments, such as beads or colorful barrettes, may be used while in uniform.

Wigs or hairpieces may be worn by either male or female soldiers, although the rules differ somewhat. For either, the hairpiece must be of a natural human-hair color. The style must comply with all regulations affecting natural hair. For male soldiers, a wig or hairpiece is allowable in uniform only when it is used to cover natural baldness or physical disfiguration.

Facial Hair

Male soldiers need to pay close attention to the sideburn and mustache regulations, as well. Sideburns must be neatly trimmed, cut straight across in a horizontal line, and no longer than the lowest part of the exterior ear opening. A mustache may be worn if neatly trimmed and tapered; it may not have a chopped-off appearance. The hair from the mustache may not cover the top lip or extend sideways beyond an imaginary line drawn vertically from the corners of the mouth.

Other than sideburns and mustaches as described above, the face must be clean shaven. Medical exceptions can sometimes be granted when an authorized medical authority (usually a doctor) prescribes beard growth as a means of treating a medical ailment. When prescribed for medical treatment, specific details must be provided, such as the length of the treatment and the necessary length that the beard should be grown (TB MED 287).

Cosmetics

Female soldiers are allowed to wear cosmetics provided they are applied conservatively and in good taste. No exaggerated makeup, extreme shades, or faddish styles will be permitted. Lipstick and nail polish colors must also be conservative; colors such as purple, gold, blue, or white cannot be worn.

Fingernails

All soldiers, male or female, must ensure that their fingernails are clean and neatly trimmed. Nails should not detract from a military appearance and should not interfere with the normal performance of duty.

THE UNIFORM

Appearance and Fit

The appearance of the uniform itself is crucial to the overall soldierly appearance of the servicemember. The uniform should be properly fitted, in good repair, and cleaned and pressed. Today's uniforms often have blouses or shirts labeled "permanent press," which should mean that no pressing is needed. If the uniform piece does not *look* pressed, however, it needs a touch-up. The soldier's appearance should leave no doubts as to the degree of self-discipline and pride he possesses.

Some general rules apply:

- Articles carried in pockets should not protrude from the pocket.
- Pockets should not be filled so full they appear bulky.
- Keys or key chains may not be attached to the belt, unless required for special duty (such as charge of quarters).
- Buttons must be buttoned; snaps, snapped; and zippers, zipped.
- All metallic parts of the uniform (such as belt buckles and belt tips) must be shined, scratch-free, and not corroded.
- Medals and ribbons must look clean and must not be frayed; they should be replaced when they look tattered or dirty.
- Shoes and boots should be shined to a high luster.
- When sleeves of jackets and coats are pressed, no crease is to be made.
- Trousers, slacks, shirts, and blouses will be creased during pressing.

The uniform must fit properly in order to look good. In addition, the Army has established definitive guidelines as to what "proper fit" means. The soldier should abide by those rules.

The black all-weather coat should have a sleeve length a ½ inch longer than the service coat worn under the all-weather coat; this means the sleeve length should be 1½ inches below the wristbone. For the male soldier, the bottom of the all-weather coat should be 1½ inches below the midpoint of the knee. For the female soldier, it should be 1 inch below the skirt length but not less than 1½ inches below the crease at the back of the knee.

The uniform coats and jackets should have a sleeve length of 1 inch below the wristbone, for any soldier.

Trousers, for all soldiers, should be fitted with the lower edge of the waistband at the top of the hipbone. A ½ inch leeway, either higher or lower, is allowed. Trousers are now allowed to have a slight break in the crease across the front, where the hem rests slightly on the shoe. This change in policy avoids the "high-water" look, in which the socks show below the trouser hem. The front crease of the trousers must reach the top of the instep; the trouser leg is then cut diagonally so that the length in the back reaches a midpoint between the top of the heel and the top of the standard shoe.

Slacks, for female soldiers, follow the same basic fitting rules as those for trousers. One exception is the waistband, which is to be worn at the natural waistline of the soldier.

Knee-length skirts have a 3-inch range in length. The shortest is to be not more than 1 inch above the crease at the back of the knee; the longest, not more than 2 inches below the crease at the back of the knee. (Note that the correct length of the all-weather black coat can be affected by the selected length of the skirt or dress.)

Appropriate undergarments are to be worn at all times with the military uniform.

To Wear or Not to Wear

Just as there are many rules on *how* to wear the uniform, there are also rules on *when* to wear it.

Generally, the Army uniform is worn while on duty. Exceptions can be made by the commander of a major command, by the Office of the Secretary of the Army, by HQDA, and by a few other high-ranking officials, but civilian clothes are authorized by these officials only when the requirements of the mission demand them. For the most part, soldiers will be in uniform while on duty.

Combining some civilian clothing with the Army uniform is not allowed. This ruling specifically excludes wearing a commercial rucksack or backpack while in uniform, unless the soldier is riding a bicycle or motorcycle at the time. Otherwise, the rucksack can only be carried in the hand.

Civilian outdoor activities, such as volksmarches or orienteering, might seem suitable times for wearing the utility or field uniform (fatigues). Army regulations specifically prohibit wearing the uniform, however, while participating in or observing such activities. The one exception is that a local commander may volunteer support personnel for such activities to serve as medical help or traffic control. The field uniform may then be the appropriate attire, at the discretion of the local commander.

Other times when the uniform may *not* be worn include when the soldier is participating in:

- Political activities.
- Commercial interests.
- Off-duty civilian employment.
- Public speeches or interviews.
- Picket lines, marches, rallies, or public demonstrations.
- Any activity that may bring discredit on the Army.

Recognized authorities can make exceptions to the wearing of the uniform during some of these activities if such actions are deemed appropriate.

Just as military regulations *prohibit* the wearing of the uniform during some activities, there are situations in which the wearing of the uniform is *required*. These include the requirement to wear either the Class A or Class B uniform (defined below; basically a uniform other than the field or utility uniform) while on a military airlift or a DOD contract flight. Wearing civilian clothing while traveling by commercial or private aircraft is allowed only when authorized by the commander. Otherwise the Class A or B uniform will be worn then as well. For overseas travel, the soldier should plan on wearing a uniform, unless he is instructed on travel orders that civilian clothing is mandatory (this decision would be made, if necessary, by the U.S. Air Foreign Clearance Guide Office).

Headgear must be worn with the uniform when the soldier is outside. Often the soldier has choices of which hat/headgear he wishes to wear with a particular uniform. That information is covered below for specific uniforms. Further details can be found in AR 670-1.

Headgear is *not required* when the soldier is indoors, in a privately owned or commercial vehicle, or in a public conveyance (such as a subway, bus, train, or plane). When the soldier is in a military vehicle, the headgear is to be worn, unless wearing the headgear interfers with safe operation of the vehicle.

Female soldiers are also permitted not to wear headgear when attending evening social events in any of the following uniforms: the Army blue, white, or green dress uniform; or the green maternity uniform.

Certain combinations of uniforms are authorized (described below by uniform; full details in AR 670-1). Mixing uniform pieces in manners not specifically authorized in the regulations is prohibited. All service uniform combinations are authorized for year-round wear. Weather conditions and assigned duties should be considered, however, when the choice of uniform is made.

Jewelry and Eyeglasses

Conservative is the key word for jewelry and eyeglasses in order for the soldier to be allowed to wear them while in uniform. Faddish or exceptionally ornamental pieces are inappropriate. For instance, eyeglasses with initials or other adornments on the lens or the frame are not authorized.

A wristwatch, an ID bracelet, and two rings may be worn while in uniform. Wedding sets are considered as one ring. Even if the jewelry is conservative and in good taste, the soldier may be prohibited from wearing it, for health or safety reasons, by the local commander. A male soldier may also wear a conservative tie tack or tie clasp with the black four-in-hand necktie. A female soldier may wear a single set of small, conservative earrings that are spherical and unadorned; are gold, silver, or white pearl; fit snugly against the ear; do not extend below the earlobe (except that nonpierced earrings may have a band extending slightly below the lobe to the back of the ear); and do not exceed ¼ inch in diameter. Earrings are not authorized with field or utility uniforms, physical fitness uniforms, or organizational uniforms such as hospital, food, or service. When earrings are worn, a matched pair is required and only one earring may be worn on each earlobe. Male soldiers may never wear earrings while in uniform.

No jewelry, watch chains, pens or pencils, or similar items can be exposed on the uniform. Exceptions: the tie tack or clasp, and exposed pens or pencils while in the hospital duty, food service, or flight uniforms.

SELECTED INDIVIDUAL UNIFORMS

To discuss fully each possible military uniform, a book twice this size would be needed—and then it would cover only uniforms. Selection of uniforms was based on those used most frequently. Some uniforms were eliminated because they were in a state of change when the book was being written; the hospital duty and food service personnel, for instance, will be getting new uniforms. The Army Clothing and Equipment Board approved the development of the new uniforms in the final months of 1985. No details were available on what changes would be made to the current uniforms.

One change that will begin surfacing sometime in 1986 is in the cold weather clothing items. The Army Natick Research and Development Center, Natick, Massachusetts, developed the new Extended Cold Weather Clothing System (ECWCS). Soldiers in the light infantry divisions will be the first to see the ECWCS. Next should be soldiers with the Special Forces, Rangers, and other units in "Climate Zone VII." Eventually, as Army stocks of current cold weather clothing items are diminished, all soldiers requiring cold weather uniforms will receive the ECWCS.

Another item recently approved by the Army Clothing Board and Army staff is the gray physical fitness uniform which replaces the black and gold version. The sweat shirt, sweat pants, shorts and athletic shirt ensemble, designed for both sexes, is more durable than the previous version. In addition, they will not shrink, fade, or lose their shape. The pants and sweatshirt have stretch material in the arm and crotch for greater comfort. This uniform is currently available in post exchanges and Army clothing sales stores. It should be a standard clothing bag item for soldiers in basic training sometime in 1988.

Airborne-qualified soldiers got a wish fulfilled early in 1986. Previously, unless assigned to an airborne unit, these soldiers could not wear their airborne insignia nor could they blouse their trousers. Under a change in the regulations, however, airborne-qualified soldiers *on jump status* in a non-airborne unit are now authorized these two privileges.

Significant changes were made affecting the wearing of the "extras" that go along with the military police (MP) MOS. The MP badge was no longer authorized to be worn on the green shirt, black all-weather coat, or utility uniform, as of January 1986. It is now restricted for wear only on the Army green service uniform coat. A subdued MP brassard (sleeve sheath) now distinguishes the MOS when the soldier is wearing the utility uniform, and the full-color brassard is used with the green shirt and black coat.

The Army changed one other policy for very practical reasons. Previously, regulations prohibited soldiers from using sew-on rank with organizational equipment and clothing items issued by a unit and turned back in to the unit when the soldier is transferred. An exception to this policy was made for the camouflage helmet cover. The pin-on rank was easily caught on camouflage nets and wire because of its sharp edges; so, the Army now allows soldiers to use subdued sew-on rank instead.

Battle Dress Uniform

The temperate and hot weather battle dress uniforms (BDUs) can be worn by all soldiers year-round, when authorized by the local commander. Even when authorized, however, they are for duty only and cannot be worn for travel or off the military installation, other than between the soldier's living quarters and duty station. BDUs are considered combat, field, training, or utility uniforms, not all-purpose uniforms. No components of the BDUs are to be intermixed with other uniforms.

BDUs are functional, loose-fitting uniforms; alterations should not be made so that the fit is tight. A tight fit reduces air flow, which is needed for ventilation and cooling through the uniform.

The coat is worn outside the trousers, but a belt is still required with the trousers. A newly styled coat is authorized in addition to the older design. The new coat has a narrower collar, narrower waist take-up tabs, and a side flare on the breast bellow pockets. Coat sleeves can be rolled, if desired; if rolled, the camouflage pattern must remain exposed and the sleeve must be above, but not more than 3 inches above, the elbow.

The trousers are to be bloused; either a draw cord or blousing rubbers are provided. If trousers are tucked inside boots, they do not have to be bloused.

BDUs are never to be starched and, by regulation, do not require pressing unless ordered by the commander for special occasions such as parades, reviews, or inspections, or for ceremonial occasions.

For most soldiers, no choice of headgear is allowed. The BDU cap is the only permissible headgear. It is to be worn straight on the head, with no hair showing under the cap on the forehead. The cap should make a line around the head that is parallel with the ground; in other words, it should be tilted neither up nor down in front. During cold weather, earflaps on the cap may be worn down, except when the wearer is in formation, if the commander has prescribed a wear policy to cover such times. Subdued insignia of grade will be worn on the cap at all times. Soldiers authorized to wear organizational berets or other organizational headgear may wear that headgear instead of the BDU cap.

If no other rain gear has been issued to the soldier, the black all-weather coat may be worn as a raincoat with the BDUs. The all-weather coat may be worn only in the garrison (on the installation), however, with the BDUs. When the cold weather camouflage coat (field jacket) is worn over the BDUs, it must be buttoned and zipped. The shirt collar must be worn inside either coat. If the field jacket is worn, the Army issue olive green scarf and black leather shell gloves may be worn, as well. In addition, female soldiers may carry a handbag when wearing the BDUs, provided the handbag is not carried outside of the garrison environment, except between living quarters and duty station.

Insignia and accouterments authorized for wear with BDUs include:

- Subdued combat and special skill badges.
- Subdued special skill and marksmanship tabs.
- Subdued identification badges.

- Brassards.
- Branch insignia.
- Combat leader's identification tab.
- Grade insignia.
- Headgear insignia.
- Subdued shoulder sleeve insignia for current organization.
- Name tape and U.S. Army distinguishing tapes.

No foreign badges, distinctive unit insignia, or regimental affiliation crests may be worn with the BDUs.

Maternity Work Uniform

The maternity counterpart to the BDU, the maternity work uniform follows the same basic regulations as those for the standard BDU, except as noted in this section. It is still to be loose-fitting. No belt is required for the trousers of the maternity uniform. In addition, since a separate field jacket is not issued for the pregnant soldier along with her maternity work uniform, she may wear her previously issued field jacket unbuttoned and unzipped if necessary.

Desert Battle Dress Uniform

The Desert Battle Dress Uniform (DBDU) is not issued to every soldier. It is issued as organizational clothing as prescribed by the commander, and is considered year-round wear. Like the BDU, it is considered a field, training, or combat uniform and should not be worn when other uniforms are more appropriate. DBDUs are not to be intermixed with other uniforms. DBDUs cannot be worn for travel, except between the soldier's living quarters and duty station.

Much like the BDUs, DBDUs are loose-fitting, and alterations to the loose fit are not authorized. The rules for blousing trousers and rolling sleeves are the same as for BDUs. Normally the shirt and trousers are required, but local commanders can vary this policy if appropriate for health, comfort, or efficiency in certain climatic conditions. Undershirts worn with the DBDUs must be brown in color.

The DBDU hat is the only choice of headgear unless special organizational headgear has been authorized. The DBDU hat is to be worn with no hair showing on the forehead, and with the chin strap pulled up under the chin.

When the parka is worn, it is to be buttoned and the shirt collar is to be inside. The olive green scarf and black leather shell gloves may be worn when the parka is used.

DBDUs have distinctive daytime and nighttime patterns.

Insignia and accouterments authorized for wear with DBDUs include:

- Subdued combat and special skill badges (pin-on only).
- Brassards.
- Branch insignia (pin-on only).
- Grade insignia.
- Headgear insignia.
- Subdued shoulder sleeve insignia for the current organization.
- Name and U.S. Army distinguishing tapes.

No foreign badges, distinctive unit insignia, or regimental affiliation crests may be worn with the BDUs.

Cold Weather Uniform

The wool OG 108 cold weather uniform is yet another organizational clothing uniform issued by local commanders when appropriate. It too can be considered a year-round utility uniform. Because it is a utility or field uniform, it is not to be worn for travel or when other uniforms are more appropriate. Distinctive from rules governing BDUs and DBDUs, components of the cold weather uniform may be worn with other utility or organizational uniforms as a cold weather ensemble when such wear is prescribed by the commander.

This uniform is also designed to be loose-fitting, and no alterations to that fit are authorized. When the OG 108 shirt is worn as an outer garment, it must be tucked inside the trousers and worn with a belt. Trousers worn as an outergarment are to be bloused. Sleeves for the cold weather uniforms may not be rolled.

Female soldiers may wear either the female OG 108 shirt or the male OG 108 shirt, depending on which is issued.

Either the BDU cap or the cold weather cap may be worn with the cold weather uniform. Organizational berets and headgear are also authorized with this uniform. Wearing of the BDU cap is to follow the same regulations as described with the BDU uniform. Rules for wearing of the cold weather cap are similar. No hair is to show below the hat on the forehead. Earflaps are always to be fastened: when worn down they are to be fastened beneath the chin, and when worn up they are to be fastened against the cap.

The olive green scarf and black leather shell gloves may be worn with any authorized outergarments for the cold weather uniform. Coats must always be buttoned or zipped, and shirt collars must be inside the coat.

Insignia and accouterments authorized for wear with the cold weather uniform include:

- Subdued combat and special skill badges (pin-on only).
- Brassards.
- Subdued branch insignia (pin-on only).
- Combat leader's identification tab (on field jackets).
- Headgear insignia.
- Name and U.S. Army distinguishing tapes.

Shoulder sleeve insignia is not authorized with the OG 108 shirts. Collar insignia, and name and U.S. Army distinguishing tapes are also not to be worn on the shirt if the shirt is authorized only as an undergarment. The name tape will not be worn on the cold weather parka (OG 107). Foreign badges, distinctive unit insignia, regimental affiliation crests, and sew-on badges and insignia of grade are not to be used with this uniform.

Army Green Service Uniform (Male)

The Army green service uniform is a versatile ensemble of uniform components that can be worn in various combinations to make a Class A uniform, a Class B uniform, or a green dress uniform. While the dress uniform is for limited occasions, the Class A and Class B uniforms can be worn year-round for a wide variety of occasions: on- or off-duty, during travel, or at private or official informal social gatherings. A number of uniform accessories can be purchased at the discretion of the soldier. Soldiers can also decide to purchase Army green service uniforms from commercial sources; it is still the responsibility of the soldier, however, to ensure that the uniform he purchases complies with all Army regulations.

The Class A uniform consists of the Army green coat and trousers, worn with either a long- or short-sleeve green shade 415 shirt and a black four-in-hand necktie. The Class B uniform omits the coat; the tie can also be omitted if the short sleeve shirt is worn. The Army green dress uniform consists of the Army green coat and trousers, with a commercially purchased long-sleeve white shirt and a black bow tie. Boots, berets, or organizational items such as brassards or MP accessories are not authorized with the dress uniform. The dress uniform cannot be worn for duty or travel. It is restricted to formal social functions, private or official, and transit to and from that function.

The Army green coat is a single-breasted, peaked lapel coat with four

Camouflage Cap

Camouflage Field Jacket

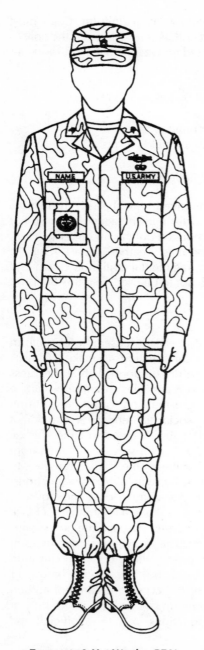

Temperate & Hot Weather BDU

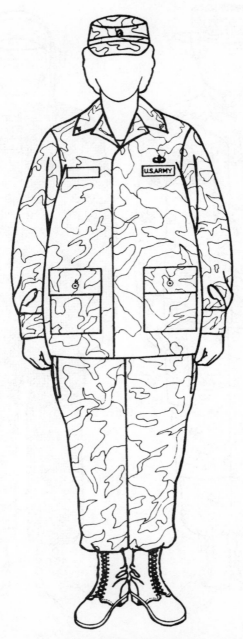

Maternity Work Uniform

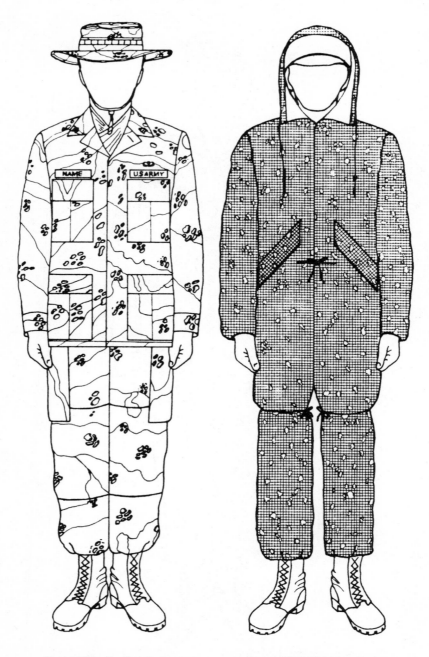

Desert BDU, Daytime Pattern   **Desert BDU, Nighttime Pattern**

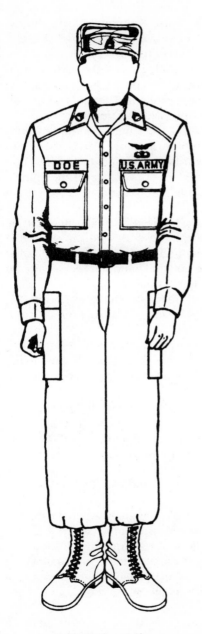

Cold Weather Uniform

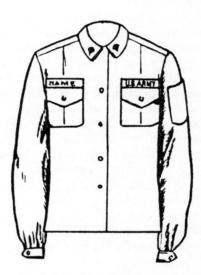

Wool Serge Shirt, Female

buttons. The fit should provide a slight drape in both the front and the back, but it should be fitted slightly at the waist. No pronounced tightness at the waist or flare below the waist is authorized. The enlisted sleeve is plain. The length of the coat will extend below the crotch.

Matching Army green trousers are straight legged, without cuffs. Trousers provide side and hip pockets; and the left hip pocket has a buttonhole tab and button (which should always be buttoned). The enlisted trouser leg is also plain. A belt must always be worn with the trousers.

The uniform shirts bear the title AG 415, whether long- or short-sleeved. Both are dress shirts; and both have shoulder loops, seven buttons, and two pockets with button-down flaps. Soldiers frequently have the flaps sewn closed to add to the military appearance of the shirt; a seamstress can carefully sew the flap along the existing seam so that the extra stitching is not apparent.

The collar of the short-sleeve shirt is a "convertible collar" that can be worn with or without a tie. If the optional pullover or cardigan sweater is worn with the short-sleeve shirt, and the tie is not worn, the shirt collar should be worn outside the sweater. The optional windbreaker can also be worn with the AG 415 sweater as the Class B uniform.

Soldiers may choose to purchase and wear an optional wool shirt, AG 428. The AG 428 is styled like the AG 415 and is available with long or short sleeves.

Both long- and short-sleeve shirts must be tucked into the trousers, whether or not the coat is worn. The shirt edge should form a straight line with the front fly opening on the trousers and the outside edge of the belt buckle. (See the illustration.)

Soldiers have a choice for headgear. The Army green garrison cap can be worn. The cap should be worn so that the front vertical crease is centered on the forehead, although the cap should have a slight tilt to the right. This tilt should not be exaggerated nor may the cap touch the top of the right ear. In addition, the crown of the cap should form a straight line. Reshaping the crown so that it peaks in the front and back and sways in the middle is not authorized wear.

If the soldier prefers, he may wear the Army green service cap. The ornamental chin strap is to remain across the visor of the cap. The service cap can be worn with either the Class A or Class B uniform. It should sit straight on the soldier's head, forming a line around the head parallel with the ground. In other words, the hat is not to be tilted to either side or to the front or back. The shape of the service cap should not be altered in any way.

Organizational berets and drill sergeant hats are also authorized headgear, except with the green dress uniform.

Accessories for the Army green uniforms consist of:

- Black web belt, with a brass or black tip.
- Black bow tie (with dress uniform only).
- Buttons.
- Solid brass belt buckle.
- Cold weather service cap (only when wearing the black all-weather coat).
- Black all-weather coat.
- Black leather unisex dress gloves (when wearing the Class A or dress uniform, the black all-weather coat, or the windbreaker).
- Military police accessories.
- Black four-in-hand necktie.
- Black scarf (with black all-weather coat or windbreaker).
- White shirt (with green dress uniform only).
- Black oxford shoes.
- Black socks.
- Black leather combat boots (not with dress uniform).
- Olive green socks when wearing combat boots.
- Black cardigan sweater.
- Black pullover sweater (with Class B uniform only).
- White undershirt.
- Black windbreaker (with Class B uniform only).

Insignia, awards, badges, and accouterments differ for wear with the Class B uniform. For the Class A and dress uniforms, the following are authorized:

- Brassards (with Class A only).
- Branch of service scarfs (with Class A only).
- Fourragère/lanyard.
- Distinctive items for infantry personnel.
- Branch insignia.
- U.S. insignia.
- Insignia of grade.
- Headgear insignia.
- Distinctive unit insignia.
- Regimental affiliation crest (required wear with the black pullover sweater).
- Combat leader's identification tab.
- OCS insignia.
- Full-color shoulder sleeve insignia for the current assignment.

- Full-color shoulder sleeve insignia for a former wartime unit.
- Nameplate.
- Organizational flash (worn only on organizational berets).
- Background trimming.
- Airborne insignia.
- Overseas service bars.
- Service stripes.
- Decoration and service medal ribbons.
- Full-size medals (dress uniform only).
- Unit awards.
- U.S. badges (full-size or miniature, for identification, marksmanship, combat, or special skills; special skill or marksmanship tabs, also).
- Foreign badges.

The authorized insignia for the Class B uniform is much more streamlined. It consists of:

- Nameplate.
- Headgear insignia.
- Insignia of grade.
- Distinctive unit insignia (worn only on the black pullover sweater).
- Decorations and awards.

Green Classic Service Uniform (Female)

The Army green classic service uniform is the servicewoman's counterpart to the Army green service uniform for the male soldier. The classic service uniform is also a versatile ensemble of components that can be arranged to form a Class A, Class B, and green dress uniform. All three uniforms can be worn year-round for a wide variety of occasions, including on- and off-duty, during travel, and for social occasions of both an official and unofficial nature. The dress uniform should be worn for formal social occasions, but any of the three are acceptable for informal social occasions. It should be noted that the servicewoman has greater flexibility in the use of the green dress uniform than the serviceman is afforded.

The Army green classic service uniform replaces several uniforms previously available to servicewomen. After September 1986 the Army green uniform and the Army green pantsuit uniform are not authorized for wear. In addition, the mint green service uniform is not authorized for wear after September 1986.

The Class A uniform consists of the Army green classic coat and either

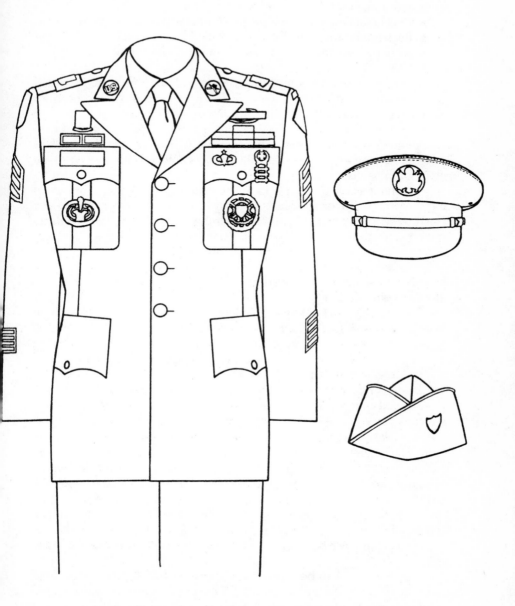

Army Green Uniform, Service Cap (top), and Garrison Cap

the Army green classic skirt or slacks, an AG 415 short- or long-sleeve shirt, and a black neck tab. For the Army green classic dress uniform, a white shirt is substituted for the green 415 shirt. Combat boots, organizational berets, and items such as brassards and MP accessories, which can be worn with the Class A or Class B uniforms, are prohibited with the classic dress uniform.

The Class B uniform omits the coat. In addition, the black neck tab can be omitted if the short-sleeve 415 shirt is worn. The white shirt is not authorized for wear with the Class B uniform.

The Army green classic coat is a hip-length, single-breasted coat with four buttons and button-down shoulder loops. Two slanted flap pockets complement the front of the coat. The collar is notched and the sleeves are plain for the enlisted servicewoman.

Matching green classic slacks are straight legged with a slight flare at the bottom. A zipper closure is located in the center front. The newer classic slacks have two side pockets, but the older classic slacks with no pockets are still authorized for wear. Pant legs are plain for enlisted soldiers.

A green classic skirt can also be worn with the uniform coat. It is a knee-length skirt, slightly flared at the hem, with a waistband and side zipper closure (left side).

The green AG 415 shirt is available in short- or long-sleeve styles. Both have a cutaway design so that they can be worn on the outside of the skirt or pants; at the soldier's option, the shirts can also be tucked into the skirt or pants. The collar on the short-sleeve shirt has been designed so that it can be worn with or without the black neck tab.

Soldiers may choose to purchase optional wool shirts, AG 428, available in both long- and short-sleeve styles. Styling on the AG 428 shirts matches that of the AG 415 shirts in all aspects except for material used.

Servicewomen may choose among three items for headgear. The Army black beret is slated for phase out, but a date had not been set as of summer 1986. It will be replaced by the Army green garrison cap, which is authorized for wear at this time. A date by which all soldiers would be required to possess the garrison cap had not been established as of summer 1986. Until a possession date is established, servicewomen cannot be required to wear the garrison cap. Since it is the coming trend, the servicewoman can enhance her professional image by switching to the cap at any time.

Garrison caps can be worn with either the Class A, Class B, or dress uniform. The cap should be worn with the front vertical crease centered on the forehead. No hair should show on the forehead below the front bottom edge of the cap, which should be situated approximately one inch above the eyebrows. (That normally corresponds to about two finger-widths above the eyebrows.) The cap will be opened on the head, so that the crown of the head is covered. The back vertical crease should fit snugly to the back of the head.

The third alternative for headgear is the green service hat. Hat insignia is to be worn with the service hat, centered on the hatband. This hat is an optional item, permissible for wear with the Class A, Class B, or dress uniform. It should be worn straight on the head so that the hatband would form a line parallel with the ground. Hair should not be visible on the forehead below the front brim of the hat. The brim should be one-half to one inch above the eyebrows (between one and two finger-widths).

Organizational berets and drill sergeant hats are also authorized for wear with the servicewoman's green classic uniform. When the classic dress uniform is worn for duty or for daytime social occasions, headgear is required. Under regulations passed early in 1986, however, the classic green dress uniform can be worn without headgear to formal evening social events.

Most of the accessories available to servicemen with their green service uniform are applicable (in female styles) for the servicewomen with their green classic uniforms. The exceptions are as follows. Servicewomen do not wear belts or buckles with the classic uniform, nor do they wear the necktie or bow tie. Their only color option for socks is black, and these can be worn only when slacks are worn. Black combat boots can be worn with slacks, provided bloused slacks are authorized by the local commander. Additional accessories available for the classic uniform are:

- Black neck tab.
- Handbags, either the black service handbag or the optional black clutch, which can be carried only with the Class A or Class B uniform.
- Black pumps (shoes).
- Sheer stockings.
- Black umbrella.

The insignia, awards, badges, and accouterments for the servicewomen's Class A and dress uniforms are the same as those allowed for the servicemen's Class A and dress uniforms, with the exceptions that servicewomen, because of MOS limitations, would not be authorized to wear distinctive items for infantry personnel or combat leader's identification tabs. Likewise, the authorized insignia for the Class B uniform is the same as those for servicemen.

Green Maternity Service Uniform

The pregnant soldier needs a special uniform and has been provided one with considerable flexibility. The ensemble of components can be combined to form all three classes of uniforms, much like the green classic service uniform. The Class A uniform is composed of a green maternity tunic, either matching maternity slacks or skirt, a long- or short-sleeve AG 415 maternity shirt, and a black neck tab. No maternity jacket is provided. For the Class B uniform, the tunic is omitted, and the neck tab may also be omitted if the short-sleeve shirt is worn. The Army green maternity dress uniform is identical to the Class A uniform except that slacks are not authorized as a maternity dress component. No white maternity shirt is available for the dress uniform. At the commander's discretion, civilian clothes may be worn for formal functions by the pregnant soldier.

Headgear rules follow the standard servicewoman's uniform regulations. No headgear is required for evening social functions with the dress uniform.

The tunic is hip length, sleeveless, and scoop-necked. It has a front inverted pleat and adjustment tabs at the waist.

Both the skirt and slacks provide a nylon knitted stretch front panel. Both have elastic waistbands, as well.

Maternity AG 415 shirts are hip length, with a straight cut bottom, since they are to be worn on the outside of the skirt or slacks. The short-sleeve shirt has a convertible collar that can be worn as a turn-down collar or closed with the neck tab. The newest maternity shirts have shoulder loops, standard with the nonmaternity servicewomen's shirts. Shirts without shoulder loops are still authorized, but kits are now available through the AAFES stores (an optional purchase item) to update the older models. Kits sold for $2.20 in January 1986 and provided two shoulder loops, two buttons, thread, and written instructions. Soldiers who choose not to modify their shirts should continue to wear pin-on rank on the shirt collar, as shown in the accompanying figures. With loops, however, shoulder marks are used as rank insignia. Since the tunic has no shoulder loops, when it is worn over the modified shirt, the loops of the shirt are buttoned over the tunic so the shoulder marks are on top.

Accessories, insignia, awards, badges, and accouterments for the maternity uniforms follow the same regulations as those for the servicewomen's Class A, Class B, and dress uniforms.

Army Blue Uniform

The Army Blue (Dress) Uniform is an optional purchase item for

Class B Army Green Uniform, Short Sleeve Shirt, With and Without Tie

Army Green Service Hat

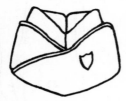

Garrison Cap

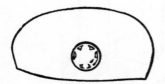

Army Black Service Beret

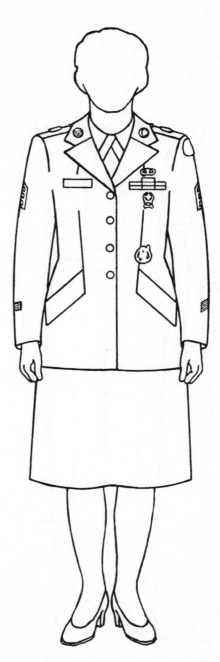

Army Green Classic Ensemble with Skirt

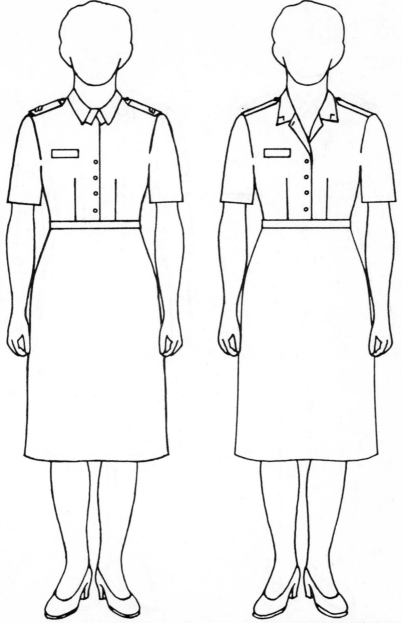

Class B Army Green Classic Ensemble, Short Sleeve Shirt, Skirt, With and Without Neck Tab

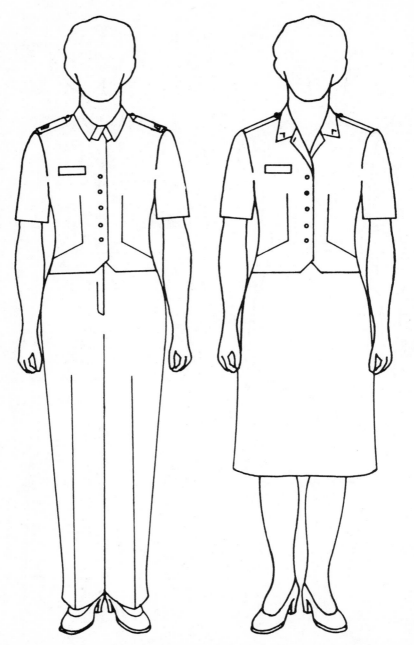

Class B Army Green Classic Ensemble, Short Sleeve Shirt and Neck Tab with Slacks, and Short Sleeve Shirt with Skirt

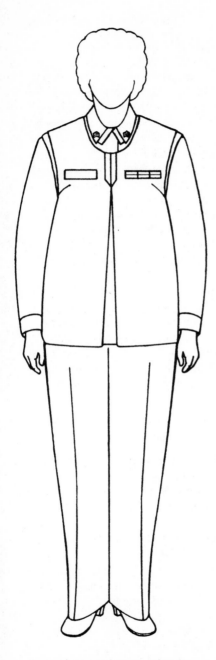

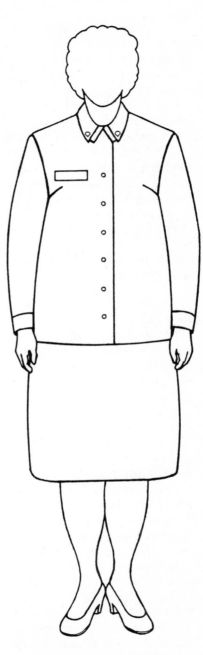

**Army Green Maternity Class A
Uniform with Pin-on Insignia**

**Army Green Maternity Class B
Uniform with Pin-on Insignia**

enlisted soldiers. When specialized units use this uniform as an organizational uniform, it will be provided to the enlisted soldier at no cost.

Normally the Army blues cannot be worn as a duty uniform (except when it is required as an organizational uniform). Its use is reserved for formal social functions, official or private, and for other appropriate occasions as desired by the individual soldier. Weddings, for example, can be an appropriate occasion for the dress blues.

The styling and fit for the jacket, trousers, and skirt are the same for the blues as they are for the Army green service uniform (for males) and the Army green classic uniform (for females). No slacks are authorized for servicewomen with the Army blue uniform. Gold ornamental braiding is included on the jacket sleeve and shoulder loops, as well as on the outside seam of the trouser legs. The trousers have both a low-waisted and high-waisted design. Servicemen use a commercially purchased long-sleeve white shirt with the dress blue uniform, while servicewomen use the military issue short-sleeve white shirt.

The accessories, insignia, awards, badges, and accouterments follow mostly the same regulations governing the wearing of the Army green dress uniforms. Differences are noted here. Gloves can be either white or black dress gloves. For servicemen, gold cuff links and studs are allowed and a choice is permitted between the black four-in-hand necktie or the black bow tie. For servicewomen, in addition to the two type of handbags that can be carried with the green dress uniform, a black fabric handbag is available.

UNIFORM ACCESSORIES

Mention is made here of a number of accessories—mostly to highlight specific regulations governing how they should be worn.

Organizational berets come in three colors: black, green, or maroon. The black is for soldiers assigned to Ranger units or to the Ranger Department of the U.S. Army Infantry School. The green signifies operational Special Forces Group personnel or soldiers who are Special Forces qualified and assigned to the U.S. Army First Special Operations Command, the U.S. Army John F. Kennedy Special Warfare Center, or the Special Operations Command for the Atlantic, Pacific, Europe, Central, or South regions. The maroon beret is for all personnel on jump status, whether assigned to airborne or non-airborne units.

The beret is to be worn so that the headband is straight across the forehead, one inch above the eyebrow. The stiffener is positioned over the left eye and the beret itself is then draped over the right ear. An adjustment ribbon is provided for correcting the size; once adjusted, however, the

Army Blue Uniform with Service Cap, Male

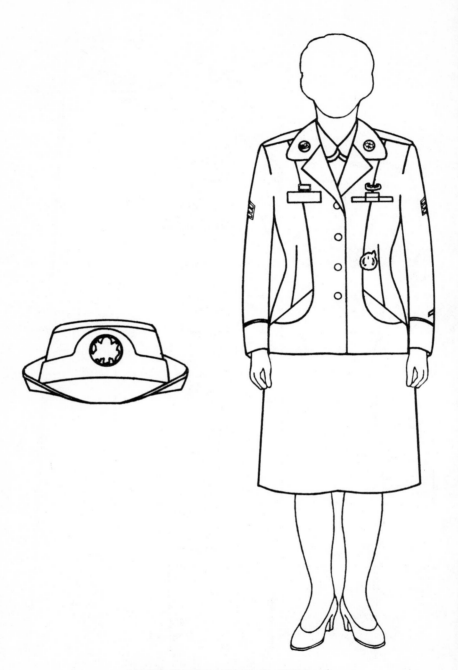

Army Blue Uniform with Service Hat, Female

ribbon should be knotted and cut, with the knot secured inside the edge binding at the back of the beret.

When organizational berets are authorized for wear, uniform trousers or slacks may be bloused if boots are also worn.

Black leather combat boots are an issue item currently undergoing revision. The newest boot has a general appearance similar to its predecessor, but the chevron tread design sole has been replaced by a deep lug tread sole. In addition the new boot has a replaceable heel, a closed loop lacing system, and a padded collar. Black laces are to be used for both boots and are to be diagonally laced. Excess laces are tucked into the top of the boot or under bloused trousers or slacks. Metal cleats and side tabs are authorized only for honor guards and ceremonial units.

Buttons are covered by regulations as well. A popular uniform button for the Army green service uniform and the Army green classic uniform is the white gold, or aluminum, button. Soldiers choosing to purchase this optional style, however, should be aware that the buttons cannot be worn after September 1989. Standard Army issue buttons are gold-colored aluminum; yellow gold buttons are optional purchase items.

Rain cap covers protect service caps from damage due to inclement weather. The transparent plastic covers can be worn with either the green or blue service caps. No covers are available for the servicewoman's green service hat.

Scarves are handy in cold weather. The black wool scarf is worn with the black all-weather coat or the windbreaker. The olive green selection is used with the cold weather utility coats (either field jackets or parkas). Both are to be folded in half lengthwise, crossed left over right at the neck, and tucked neatly into the neckline of the outergarment.

Sweaters are optional purchase items, available in cardigan or pullover styles. The cardigan can be worn as an outergarment only in the immediate work area. It cannot be worn off-post or when traveling to and from living quarters—unless it is worn under a service jacket or windbreaker and is not visible. Previously, medical personnel had an exception to this rule, but that was revoked early in 1986. The pullover style can be worn as an outergarment with the Class B uniform. When used as an outergarment, the sweater must be worn with shoulder marks indicating rank (if corporal or higher), nameplate (centered above the patch), and unit crest if one is authorized. Sleeves on uniform sweaters are never to be worn rolled or pushed up.

Windbreakers are another optional purchase item. They can be used as an outergarment with Class B uniforms in addition to the hospital duty and food service uniforms. The zipper is to be worn zipped at least three-fourths of the way up. Nonsubdued pin-on rank insignia is used with the

Cardigan Sweater, Male

Cardigan Sweater, Female

Windbreaker

Pullover Sweater

Organizational Baseball Cap

Drill Sergeant Hat, Male

Helmet Cover

Drill Sergeant Hat, Female

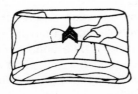

BDU Cap

Organizational Beret

windbreaker. With the rank insignia removed, it may be worn with civilian clothing.

FINISHING TOUCHES

The uniform isn't complete without the finishing touches added by the insignia, badges, awards and decorations, and the "catch-all" accouterments. Again, space limitations make a full discussion of all possible uniform pieces impractical. This reference book would not be complete without some guidance on the use of the generalized and specialized "icing to the cake."

Insignia of grade are required for all soldiers. An illustration of the insignia for enlisted personnel is provided. While the symbols of grade are always the same, the insignia themselves come in a variety of styles. Embroidered sew-on insignia are used on each sleeve of the Army green coat and the dress blue coat. Centered between the shoulder seam and the elbow of the sleeve, the insignia should have a background color that matches the coat to which it is sewn. Nonsubdued (shiny) pin-on insignia are required on the collars of the black all-weather coat, the windbreaker, and the hospital duty and food service uniforms. Enlisted personnel grade Specialist Four and below will wear the nonsubdued insignia on the collar of the AG 415 shirt as well. In each case the insignia are worn on both collars, one inch up from the collar point, with the center line of the insignia bisecting the points of the collar. Subdued pin-on insignia, used for utility uniform shirts and cold weather coats, are positioned in the same manner.

Shoulder marks are used with the AG 415 shirt for enlisted personnel grade Corporal and above. When wearing the black pullover sweater, all personnel use shoulder marks to identify their grade. Shoulder marks are slipped over the shoulder loops so that the bottom of the insignia is closest to the shoulder. Soldiers can choose between two sizes so that the fit is appropriate to the shoulder width.

Branch insignia are required for all enlisted personnel. The branch identifying symbol is placed over a plain disk. To maintain the soldierly appearance, branch insignia should be cleaned and shined frequently. Separating the insignia from the disk before cleaning ensures that no cleaning materials are left embedded in the crevices. Branch insignia should be worn on the left collar of the green or blue uniform coat. It should be placed one inch above the notch, and the centerline of the insignia should be parallel with the inside edge of the collar. A plain disk with the initials "U.S." is worn in a similar manner on the right collar.

Shoulder sleeve insignia (SSI) come in two authorized forms. The

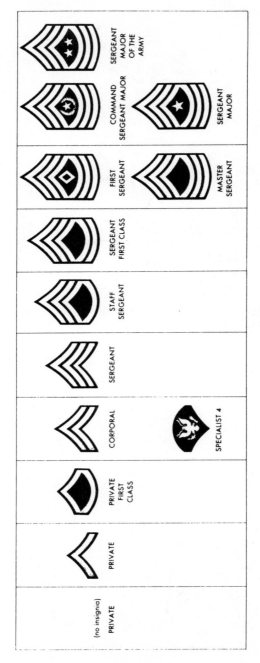

Army Ranks

Distinctive Items Authorized for Infantry Personnel

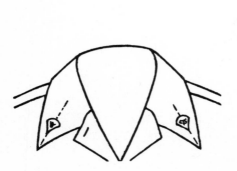

Polished Pin-on Insignia of Grade on Collars

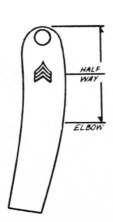

HALF
WAY

ELBOW

Sew-on Insignia of Grade

Insignia of Branch and U.S. on Army Green and Blue Uniforms

Insignia of Branch and U.S. on Army Green Classic Ensemble

Adjutant General's Corps

Air Defense Artillery

Armor

Branch Immaterial

Aviation

Cavalry

Chaplain Assistant

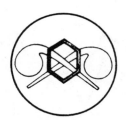

Chemical Corps

Civil Affairs

Corps of Engineers

Field Artillery

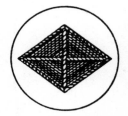

Finance

Branch Insignia

Infantry

Inspector General

Judge
Advocate General

Medical Corps

Military Intelligence

Military Police Corps

Ordnance Corps

Quartermaster Corps

Signal Corps

Special Operations

Transportation Corps

Branch Insignia

The Sergeant Major
of the Army

nonsubdued insignia for the soldier's current organization is to be worn on the left sleeve of the Army green or dress blue coat, one-half inch below the top shoulder seam. If a special identifying tab for Ranger, Special Forces, or President's Hundred is worn, it is placed in the normal position for the SSI; the SSI is then positioned one-quarter inch below the tab. Subdued insignia is worn in the same position, but on utility uniforms.

SSI for former wartime service is worn on the right shoulder of the same coats, if appropriate. (Service in Grenada, Green Island, or Carriacoa Island, between 24 October 1983 and 21 November 1983, qualifies as wartime service.) Soldiers should follow details in AR 670-1 in determining which unit insignia to wear. Nonsubdued and subdued insignia are used in the same manner as the current organization insignia.

Certain soldiers are authorized to wear the *combat leader's identification tab* but only during those times in their career when they are actually filling the command position. At the unit level, the first sergeant, platoon sergeant, section leader, squad leader, tank commander, and rifle squad fire team leader can all wear the green cloth loop. Centered on both shoulder loops, the tab is worn with the Army green coat and the cold weather coat (field jacket).

Distinctive unit insignia are used to promote esprit de corps among brigades, divisions, regiments, battalions, schools, or major commands. This insignia is worn in several locations on the uniform. It is to be centered above the nameplate when the black pullover sweater is worn; centerd on the "left curtain" on the garrison cap, one inch from the crease; centered on the organizational flash of the organizational beret; and centered on the shoulder loops of the service uniforms. If shoulder marks (rank) are worn on the loops, the DUI is to be centered between the bottom of the rank insignia and the shoulder seam. The DUI can be centered on the combat leader's identification tab as well.

Nameplates, either glossy or nonglossy, are required with most uniforms; name tapes are used when nameplates are not.

Other common uniform items are *service stripes,* one authorized for each three years of service, and *overseas service bars,* one authorized for each six months of overseas service during war. The Grenada dates do not apply; the last date to earn an overseas service bar in recent history was 1973, for service in Vietnam, Laos, or Cambodia.

Ribbons and medals are the grand finale to the soldier's professional appearance. He should rightfully feel proud of the accomplishments the ribbons represent. Consequently, it is imperative that the ribbons and medals be kept in impeccable condition. If they become soiled, they should be replaced. Ribbons should always be worn in the order of precedence, from right to left, with highest precedence ribbons in the top row (a list follows for reference). Up to four ribbons can be worn in a single row; a second row cannot be started until the soldier has earned the fourth ribbon. The first two rows are block-style with either three or four ribbons in each, but subsequent rows can be stair-stepped to the right (flush left) if the soldier chooses. When a soldier has many ribbons, this is frequently done so that the coat collar does not cover some of the awards. The top row of ribbons can either be flush left (with the stair-step pattern) or centered over the row below it (with the block-style pattern). Ribbons are worn with the Army green service uniforms and the Army blues, and are always worn on the left-hand side.

Order of precedence for ribbons is as follows (in categories or classifications of ribbon types): U.S. military decorations, U.S. unit awards, U.S. nonmilitary awards, Good Conduct Medal, U.S. campaign and service medals, U.S. service and training ribbons, U.S. Merchant Marine awards, foreign military decorations, foreign unit awards, and non-U.S. service awards. Lists follow for major categories, showing order of precedence for individual ribbons within the group.

Full-size decorations and service medals are presented to the soldier in addition to the uniform ribbon that represents the decoration or medal. Often the full-size honors end up in a display case hung on the wall. They can be worn, however, on the dress blue or dress green uniform at social functions. Miniature decorations, replicas made to a one-half scale, are optional purchase items; miniatures can be worn only on dress blues or on formal civilian attire, if such attire is appropriate for the social function. No miniature exists for the Medal of Honor. Full-size or miniature decorations are worn on the left side—breast pocket (male soldiers) or left side, centered (female soldiers) for full-size; lapel (male soldiers) or left side, centered (female soldiers) for miniatures. Up to seven miniatures can be worn in a single row, overlapping the medal on the right by up to 50 percent. The Medal of Honor is handled uniquely. It is worn on a neckband ribbon, outside the shirt collar but inside the coat collar. Marksmanship badges or Driver and Mechanic badges are not worn with either full-size or miniature decorations. Any other special skill badges must be in miniature size if miniature decorations are used.

U.S. Military Decorations

1. Medal of Honor
2. Distinguished Service Cross
3. Navy Cross
4. Air Force Cross
5. Defense Distinguished Service Medal

6. Distinguished Service Medal
7. Silver Star
8. Defense Superior Service Medal
9. Legion of Merit
10. Distinguished Flying Cross
11. Soldier's Medal
12. Navy and Marine Corps Medal
13. Airman's Medal
14. Coast Guard Medal
15. Bronze Star Medal
16. Purple Heart
17. Defense Meritorious Service Medal
18. Meritorious Service Medal
19. Air Medal
20. Joint Service Commendation Medal
21. Army Commendation Medal
22. Navy Commendation Medal
23. Air Force Commendation Medal
24. Coast Guard Commendation Medal
25. Joint Service Achievement Medal
26. Army Achievement Medal
27. Navy Achievement Medal
28. Air Force Achievement Medal
29. Coast Guard Achievement Medal
30. Combat Action Ribbon

U.S. Unit Awards

1. Presidential Unit Citation (Army & Air Force)
2. Presidential Unit Citation (Navy)
3. Joint Meritorious Unit Award
4. Valorous Unit Award
5. Meritorious Unit Commendation (Army)
6. Navy Unit Commendation
7. Air Force Outstanding Unit Award
8. Coast Guard Unit Commendation
9. Army Superior Unit Award
10. Meritorious Unit Commendation (Navy)
11. Air Force Organizational Excellence Award
12. Coast Guard Meritorious Unit Commendation

U.S. Service Medals

1. American Defense Service Medal
2. Women's Army Corps Service Medal
3. American Campaign Medal
4. Asiatic-Pacific Campaign Medal
5. European-African-Middle Eastern Campaign Medal
6. World War II Victory Medal
7. Army of Occupation Medal
8. Medal for Humane Action
9. National Defense Service Medal
10. Korean Service Medal
11. Antarctica Service Medal
12. Armed Forces Expeditionary Medal
13. Vietnam Service Medal
14. Humanitarian Service Medal
15. Armed Forces Reserve Medal
16. Army Reserve Components Achievement Medal
17. NCO Professional Development Ribbon
18. Army Service Ribbon
19. Overseas Service Ribbon
20. Army Reserve Components Overseas Training Ribbon

7

Finance

"Pay day" for the soldier comes, at most, twice a month. Usually it means longer check-cashing lines in the post exchange, longer checkout lines in the commissary, and larger crowds at the clubs. What it should involve, but frequently doesn't, is a few moments to review the Leave and Earnings Statement (LES) for accuracy.

Ultimately, you are responsible for your own financial affairs. The computerized Army pay system is generally very accurate. But with the diversified pay allowances and changing duty status among numerous soldiers handled by each Finance and Accounting Office (FAO), mistakes can occur. The sooner an error is spotted, the easier it is to correct— whether the error be an overpayment or an underpayment.

A regular review of information provided on the LES should also include checking calculations of leave. Each month the LES shows how many days of leave were used and the balance remaining at that time. Any discrepancies should be brought immediately to the attention of the FAO or your First Sergeant. More information on leave records and types of leave is presented later in this chapter.

Understanding the LES and pay entitlements and allowances is of benefit to each soldier. In addition, "knowing the system" can be invaluable. For instance, you should be aware of your choices of when to be paid, how to be paid, and to whom the pay can be disbursed. The general guidelines provided here are a starting point for verifying the accuracy of the LES and for ensuring that you are receiving all entitlements and allowances you should be. Specific details on the amount of the entitlement and instructions for completing necessary forms should be obtained from your FAO.

You're probably already aware that you can choose to be paid either once or twice a month. Midmonth payments, disbursed on the fifteenth of the month, can be in any amount you specify, up to one-half of your monthly basic pay. The remainder of your pay is disbursed on the last day of the month.

You may not be aware of all of the payment choices that are available to you. Paychecks can be disbursed in several ways. Payments can be made to you in cash or by check. Checks can be delivered to you at your unit or at another address. In addition, checks can be made payable to another individual (a dependent) or financial institution (through allotments), at an address other than your unit. If you choose, you may combine two of the payment methods in any designated dollar amounts.

Your basic pay is determined by your rank and the amount of time on active duty. A basic pay table is listed. As with any salary information, however, it will become quickly outdated. Current pay schedules are frequently available through military-oriented magazines and through insurance firms. Post newspapers and *Army Times* publish updated versions as well. Or you can check with your FAO for the current rate. When you are promoted, you should take extra care in checking the monthly LES to ensure the appropriate raise is credited on the correct date.

Monthly Basic Pay

Grade	Under 2	2	3	4	6
E-6	$965.40	$1052.40	$1096.20	$1143.00	$1185.30
E-5	847.20	922.50	966.90	1009.20	1075.20
E-4	790.50	834.60	883.50	952.20	989.70
E-3	744.60	785.10	816.90	849.30	849.30
E-2	716.40	716.40	716.40	716.40	716.40
E-1	639.00	639.00	639.00	639.00	639.00

In addition to basic pay, you can receive monthly pay entitlements, for a variety of duties or duty stations; periodic pay entitlements, for events such as a change of station or a reenlistment; and monthly allowances, for such items as clothing, subsistence, and quarters. Each is explained below.

MONTHLY PAY ENTITLEMENTS

Many forms of monthly pay entitlements are available to compensate you for special skills, for enduring hardships, or for exposure to danger. Compensation may be granted based on rank and time in service, or on time spent performing special skills or enduring hardships; or it may be standard for all individuals serving in that particular capacity. The FAO can advise you on the current compensation for each entitlement you should be receiving. You should ensure that your LES reflects all appropriate entitlements.

Special Duty Assignment Pay: $110–$220

Recruiters, drill sergeants, and career counselors receive special duty assignment pay for the service they render to the Army. If the soldier does not spend the full month in a designated special duty position, the pay is prorated for the percentage of the month actually spent performing the special duty. While the MOSs listed require some special qualifications, they are volunteer-type duties, for which the Army awards extra compensation. (See the section on reenlistment bonuses in chapter 9.)

Foreign Duty Pay (FDP): $8–$22.50

When enlisted soldiers are assigned to arduous duty stations outside the Continental United States (CONUS), they receive extra compensation in the form of FDP. Arduous duty stations have been defined as those areas where:

- Dependents are not authorized. (A soldier with no dependents serving in such an area is still entitled to FDP.)
- Dependents are authorized but the accompanied tour length is less than 36 months. (The qualifying factor is the duty assignment; not dependent status.)
- The climate is extreme. (Specific guidelines include assignments located at or above a latitude of 58° north, at or below a latitude of 58° south, and between latitudes 15° north and 15° south—in

other words, extremely cold climates near the polar regions or extremely hot climates near the equator.

Soldiers cannot receive both FDP and Sea Duty Pay, nor can they receive FDP if they are assigned to a qualifying duty station that is also their home of record.

Sea Duty Pay (SDP): $50–$410

Soldiers, in addition to sailors, can go to sea. While these assignments do not abound in the Army, when a soldier is assigned to a ship and is in a sea duty status, he is entitled to extra pay. The soldier, together with the unit commander (skipper), provides documentation to the Sea Service Office (SSO), Fort Eustis, Virginia. SDP is prorated, based on the number of days creditable sea duty and the number of consecutive months of sea duty the soldier has currently completed. A Sea Pay Monthly Premium of $100 is paid to soldiers spending more than 36 months of consecutive duty at sea.

Hostile Fire Pay (HFP): $65

National defense, the true "business" of the Army, sometimes means that soldiers are subjected to hostile fire or are stationed permanently or temporarily in an area designated as a hostile fire area. As a partial compensation for the danger the soldier is exposed to, he receives HFP for any month in which at least part of the time was served in a hostile fire area. A soldier on TDY orders for less than 30 days in a hostile fire area must submit a letter requesting the credit for HFP to his commander for approval. The letter should provide the soldier's social security number, TDY Special Order number, and a description of the tactical or strategic combat organization in which the soldier participated, or the circumstances under which he was subjected to hostile fire.

Diving Duty Pay: $175–$300

To qualify for diving duty pay, a soldier must be a rated diver serving in an assignment designated on the manpower documents as a diving position of MOS 00B or 7242. If the duty has not been designated as a diving position, approval for that designation can be routed through HQDA (DAFD-ZA), Washington, DC 20310.

Overseas Extension Pay: $80/month or 30 days' leave

Qualified enlisted soldiers serving in designated locations overseas can extend their tours overseas for either additional special pay or for extra leave. The minimum length of the extension is usually 12 months. It should be noted that not all soldiers qualify for this benefit. The First Sergeant or FAO of an overseas unit would be a good source of information for the young soldier checking into the MOSs that currently are included under this regulation. (See *Volunteering* in Chapter 5.)

Flight Pay: $83–$131

Enlisted soldiers serving either as crewmembers with flying status or non-crewmembers with flying status are eligible for flight pay, considered a form of Hazardous Duty Incentive Pay (HDIP). Both crewmembers and non-crewmembers must be performing duties essential to the mission of the aircraft and duties that can be performed only during flight. Non-crewmembers must be performing duties that cannot be performed by regular crewmembers, in order to qualify for the special pay.

Parachute Duty Pay: $83–$155

Another form of HDIP, parachute duty pay is authorized for soldiers who are students at a parachute or airborne school or at the John F. Kennedy Center for Military Assistance (if performing parachute duty), and for soldiers performing the duties of a parachutist at either an airborne unit, a non-airborne unit with a designated parachutist position, a school, or a service test section. Parachutists also receive the pay when they serve in a designated position at an approved quartermaster airborne facility concerned with maintenance, testing, and/or parachute packing and rigging, or when they serve with a pararescue team.

Demolition Pay: $83

Soldiers whose primary duty assignments involve the demolition of explosives are eligible for demolition pay. This HDIP is reserved for students or instructors in specific schools who have the Special Skill Identifier (SSI) 75D or who have the MOS 55D; or for soldiers with either the SSI or MOS, assigned to manpower positions in units or sections approved or designated as Explosive Ordnance Disposal Activities. Soldiers holding the SSI 75D or MOS 55D who work temporarily in the demoliton of explosives, or who perform the work as an additional duty, also are eligi-

Paratrooper

ble for the pay. Qualifying schools are the U.S. Naval School Explosive Ordnance Disposal, the U.S. Naval Ordnance Station, Indian Head, Maryland, or the U.S. Army Missile and Munitions Center and School, Redstone Arsenal, Alabama. Soldiers do not have to work in explosive demolition for a full month to receive the incentive pay for that month.

Experiment Stress Pay: $83

When soldiers are assigned to experimental stress duty where they are involved with thermal stress experiments or pressure chamber experiments, they receive special pay. They do not have to be involved with the experimentation for a full month to receive incentive pay for that month. Laboratories authorized to perform thermal stress experiments with human subjects are the U.S. Army Natick Laboratory, Natick, Massachusetts; the U.S. Army Chemical Research and Development Laboratory, Edgewood Arsenal, Maryland; and the U.S. Medical Research Laboratory, Ft. Knox, Kentucky. The Natick Laboratory is also designated as a site for experimental pressure chamber work with human test subjects, in addition to the Armed Forces Institute of Pathology, Washington, DC.

Toxic Fuels (or Propellants) Pay: $83

Duty involving toxic fuels or propellants also results in HDIP, but as with other HDIPs, the duty must be designated by official manpower documents.

Dual Incentive Pay

The Army recognizes that a soldier may be serving simultaneously in more than one form of hazardous duty. In such cases, dual incentive pay may be applicable, but the dual pay can be authorized only by HQDA (DAPC-ZA), Washington, DC 20310. Soldiers serving in two forms of hazardous duty should request their FAO to submit necessary forms to receive authorization.

MONTHLY ALLOWANCES

In addition to basic pay and monthly pay entitlements, you also receive monthly allowances. Allowances are really just another form of pay, but with one significant advantage—they are not taxable. These entitlements are meant to cover specific needs such as food, clothing expenses, and housing. When the government fulfills the need for you, the allowance is not awarded. For instance, soldiers living in the barracks are provided their housing. Consequently, they are not eligible for a housing allowance.

The various types of allowances and qualifications for receiving the allowance are specified below.

Basic Allowance for Subsistence (BAS)

Commonly called "separate rations," BAS is restricted to cases when a government "mess hall" is not available and when no rations are provided to the soldier. When a soldier is authorized to live off-post (see BAQ below), he will usually be awarded BAS as well. BAS is normally awarded during the time in which the soldier is on leave and during authorized travel time for PCS moves. The daily per diem rate is normally reduced, however, by the daily BAS rate. After a PCS, the soldier should verify with his new FAO whether BAS will be awarded at the new assignment. Authorization forms must be completed with each new unit.

BAS does not provide for the soldier to "eat high off the hog." Actually, the daily rates were based on cost to the government to provide meals for the soldier through quantity purchasing and preparation. Rates in effect as of January 1986:

- When rations in kind are not available—$5.89.
- When on leave, or when granted permission to mess separately—$5.21.
- When assigned under emergency conditions where no government messing is available—$7.80.

Basic Allowance for Quarters (BAQ)

Commonly called the "housing allowance," BAQ is intended to compensate soldiers who do not have housing provided by the government. Three categories have been established:

- Soldiers with dependents. If government housing is not provided for the soldier and dependents, BAQ is awarded to help offset the cost of renting in the civilian community.
- Soldiers (without dependents) living in government barracks or quarters. A small BAQ is provided to compensate partially for the inconveniences of living in a barracks situation. This token BAQ is called a partial rate.

- Soldiers (without dependents) living off-post. BAQ is less than the rate for soldiers of the same rank who have dependents; it is considerably more, however, than the partial rate.

For Army couples, when both spouses are servicemembers, the guidelines change somewhat. If the couple has children, the soldier with the highest rank will receive BAQ at the "with dependents" rate; the spouse will receive BAQ at the "without dependents" rate. In addition, if the couple has no children each spouse will receive the BAQ without dependents rate.

When government quarters on post are provided to families, the soldier forfeits his BAQ. Since BAQ covers only part of housing costs, using government quarters can be a significant savings. Some government quarters are not "up to par," however, and have been rated substandard by the government. In these cases, the soldier forfeits only a percentage of the BAQ and in essence pays a reduced rent for the substandard housing.

BAQ Rates (January 1986)

Pay Grade	Without Dependents Full Rate	Partial Rate	With Dependents
E-6	$228.00	$9.90	$348.00
E-5	210.90	8.70	309.30
E-4	183.00	8.10	267.30
E-3	177.60	7.80	245.70
E-2	150.90	7.20	245.70
E-1	137.40	6.90	245.70

Special Allowances

BAQ and BAS are monthly allowances provided for subsistence, or food and housing. The Army also provides a number of special allowances that are not necessarily paid on a monthly basis.

Family Separation Allowances (FSA) cover two specific situations that increase the cost of housing for the soldier with dependents. First, if the soldier is assigned overseas to an area where dependents are not authorized, and if no government quarters are available to that soldier, he will receive an FSA equivalent to the BAQ of a soldier without dependents. This FSA is in addition to the soldier's standard BAQ to provide housing for dependents. FSA is also awarded when the soldier with dependents is either overseas, in a dependent-restricted area, where quarters are provided, or when he is on temporary duty away from the family for 30 days or more. In both cases the FSA is $30 per month.

Variable Housing Allowances (VHA) help offset the cost of housing in areas where rent is higher than the national average. Many areas provide no VHA. This monthly allowance is still provided to soldiers stationed overseas when their families are living in a high-cost area in the United States.

Station Housing Allowances (SHA) are similar to VHAs except that they are awarded for overseas areas. In addition, Advance Station Housing Allowance (ASHA) is paid to help the soldier with the high costs of securing housing overseas, covering such costs as paying advanced rent and security deposits. The ASHA must be repaid, but it can be prorated over a 12-month period.

Rent-Plus is another method of supplementing the housing expenses overseas. Under this program the actual expenses of the soldier are considered, including rent, average utility costs, and additional costs associated with an overseas lease. Not all overseas areas have the Rent-Plus allowance.

Cost-of-Living Allowances (COLA) are yet another allowance for soldiers stationed outside of the United States. COLA is meant as a means of repaying the soldier for the excess costs of living in the overseas area. It does not relate solely to housing. Therefore, soldiers living in the barracks overseas are still awarded COLA but at a reduced rate of 47 percent of the daily COLA rate for a soldier without dependents.

Dislocation Allowances are one-time payments, equal to a month's BAQ, to help defray the costs of moving, when the move is within CONUS. Soldiers with dependents always receive the allowance with a PCS; soldiers without dependents receive the allowance only if they were entitled to BAQ at both the previous and the new duty assignment. Dislocation allowances are taxable, however.

Temporary Lodging Allowances (TLA) are also used for soldiers moving from one duty assignment to another. The TLA is determined for each area, based on cost of living. Its purpose is to partially reimburse the soldier for extra expenses incurred through the necessity of using temporary quarters that do not provide facilities for preparing meals. The daily rate, usually not authorized for more than 60 days, is determined in part by the number of dependents. Single soldiers usually receive one-half of the local per diem rate.

Per Diem is a daily allowance provided for soldiers working on temporary duty away from their normal duty station. It covers both housing and meals, although realistically it is often insufficient to fully cover the costs of motels and restaurant dining. The maximum per diem rate in the United States is $75 per day; overseas area can be as high as $200 per day.

The *Clothing Maintenance Allowance* (CMA) is provided for the general upkeep and maintenance of the service uniform. This small monthly payment carries with it an unspoken obligation—to keep the uniform in a soldierly appearance. (See chapter 6 for more details.) For the first 36 months on a military career, the soldier receives a Basic CMA; he then switches to a higher CMA Standard.

Other clothing allowances are also possible. If the soldier is required to work in civilian clothes, in investigative work, for instance, or in some designated overseas areas, he is provided a one-time *Special Clothing Allowance* (SCA) intended for the purchasing of new civilian clothing. This is not a monthly allowance as is the CMA. While on temporary duty to an area where civilian clothes are required, soldiers are also eligible to receive the SCA.

REENLISTMENT BONUSES

In its complex pay system the Army offers one more type of pay—bonuses. Theoretically, a soldier can earn up to $8,000 in Reenlistment Bonuses during his entire career, and up to $30,000 in Selective Reenlistment Bonuses, which are awarded in critical MOSs. Both amounts are the legal maximum that can be paid to any one soldier. Few soldiers even come close to that maximum.

Bonuses are used to encourage the reenlistment of dedicated soldiers. Reenlistment bonuses have been limited in recent years to soldiers in the combat arms field. Other career fields, however, are also offered reenlistment bonuses from time to time. The best source of information on reenlistment is your career counselor.

LEAVE

Even before entering the Army, the prospective soldier learns about the vacation benefits the military offers. Called "leave" in military jargon, the soldier knows his benefit—30 days a year, far more than most civilian employers. That is not, however, the full picture. Many soldiers are not aware of the full range of leaves and passes through which they can be excused from their normal duty and still receive their full pay.

The 30 days of *annual leave* are earned at a rate of 2.5 days per month, whether the soldier is an active duty member or an Army Reserve or National Guard member serving full-time on active duty during a given

30-day period. The soldier draws against his "accrued leave" much in the same way he would draw against an accrued (saved) balance in a banking account. The "bank statement" for annual leave is shown on the LES. (As mentioned previously, it is your responsibility to monitor the statement for accuracy of the entries.) Unlike a savings account in a bank, however, the soldier is not allowed to accrue more than 60 days of leave, unless in a combat zone, where the ceiling is increased to 90 days.

Under a few conditions the soldier will not earn the designated 2.5 days a month, but all are disciplinary or misconduct causes. Briefly, if the soldier is AWOL, confined by military or civilian authorities, or away from duty and in excess leave, he does not earn further leave during that period.

Annual leave is the 30 days of ordinary leave a soldier can accrue annually. A DA Form 31 must be filled out and signed by the soldier's commander authorizing the absence from work. Rarely would annual leave requests be disapproved in conjunction with a PCS move. (Travel time granted with a PCS move does not count against the soldier's accrued leave.) Annual leave is often requested (and approved) when the soldier is already going to be away from the duty station for temporary duty. Commanders try to approve any leave requests that do not present a conflict with the needs of the Army.

Advance leave is like a loan—the soldier is requesting to take more from his account than is presently there. Commanders can approve advance leave when the soldier has enough time remaining before ETS to reasonably repay the advance.

Emergency leave is charged against the soldier's accrued leave or is granted as advance leave if an adequate amount of accrued leave is not available. When an emergency situation arises, such as the death of a family member, a dying family member, an illness in an immediate family member where the presence of the servicemember is deemed essential, or under circumstances where the absence of the soldier causes severe or unusual hardship on the family, the emergency must be verified by the American Red Cross. The commander is then authorized to approve emergency leave.

If the soldier is overseas and must travel back to the United States to handle the emergency situation, the first part of the trip (to an international airport within the United States) is government-paid transportation. If the soldier must travel from the United States to an overseas location, travel from the international airport is at government expense. Soldiers traveling from one overseas location to another overseas location have the full trip at government expense, even if part of the trip must be in the United States. For instance, if the soldier is in Europe and must travel to the Pacific, travel from Europe to the U.S. East Coast, then from the East Coast to the West

Coast, and finally from the West Coast to the Pacific location will all be government-paid transportation.

These same travel benefits apply to dependents as well, whether or not they are traveling with the servicemember. No travel benefits are available for soldiers stationed in the United States who must travel to another U.S. location on emergency leave.

Convalescent leave is not charged against a soldier's accrued leave, nor is it considered an advance leave. This leave is granted by hospital commanders to patients who need the extra time for rehabilitation or recuperation. Basically, they are well enough to be discharged from the hospital but not yet ready to resume duty.

Graduation leave is available at the discretion of the commander for graduates of the U.S. Military Academy upon their commissioning. It is not charged against accrued leave. (See chapter 9 for details on the possibility of attending the Military Academy.)

Special leave is granted to some soldiers who extend their overseas assignments. Not all overseas locations qualify, and soldiers must have certain MOS ratings. The First Sergeant or the FAO overseas can provide current information. Generally this nonchargeable 30-day leave is reserved for combat arms MOSs. The special leave is a matter of choice for the soldier. Granting special leave negates eligibility for overseas extension pay.

Another limited overseas program is the *Environmental and Moral Leave* (EML) Program, applicable to 57 underdeveloped or Communist-controlled countries. While leave is chargeable under the EML Program, transportation costs for the soldier and dependents to a designated "relief destination" are paid by the government; and travel time is not chargeable as leave. Areas chosen for this program by the Department of Defense are selected because of the unusually difficult living conditions, which cause excessive physical and mental discomfort. The program is designed to provide temporary relief to avoid a "deleterious effect" on the soldier.

Soldiers and their families stationed in the South American countries of Belize, Bolivia, Columbia, El Salvador, Guatemala, Honduras, Paraguay, or Peru can travel to Miami; those in Burma, Indonesia, Malaysia, Nepal, Sri Lanka, or Thailand can travel to Hong Kong; if stationed in the People's Republic of China, soldiers and dependents can travel to Malaysia; and finally, military families in Argentia, Canada can receive government-paid transportation to New York City.

Rest and Recuperation Leave (R&R) is available to soldiers serving in areas authorized to award hostile fire pay. R&R is also chargeable leave, but the leave offers a rest period for the soldier serving in a difficult situation.

PASSES

Passes differ from leave in two respects. First, they are not chargeable against your accrued leave or as advance leave. In addition, they are granted only for short periods of time.

The regular pass is limited to a maximum of three days (72 hours). Basically, it covers your normal off-duty time on weekends and holidays. Under certain circumstances, the regular pass can be rescinded.

Special passes, limited to a maximum of four days (96 hours) are rewards given to deserving soldiers for exceptional service. Frequently they are granted to the Soldier of the Month or the Soldier of the Quarter, for example. In addition, they can be used to allow a soldier to participate in religious retreats or events, to handle personal problems, or to compensate him for required duty that has extended over an unusually long period of time.

OTHER FINANCIAL MATTERS

Not only can you draw advance leave under certain circumstances, there are also situations in which you can draw advance pay. Up to three months of your basic pay is authorized as advance pay when you make a PCS move. Only one month can be granted at the old duty station or en route to the new duty station if those moneys were not anticipated and requested from the old duty station. Two additional months can be granted by the FAO at the new duty station, if the advance pay is approved by your new commander. A DA Form 2142 (Pay Inquiry) is used.

Since advance pay is a debt that must be repaid, you must have adequate time remaining before your ETS to reimburse the Army. The debt will be repaid over a maximum of one year and will be automatically deducted from your pay. The LES will document the payments.

Advance pay is not your right for each PCS. It is granted on a case-by-case basis, where you must explain the specific need for the extra funds. Such funds are in addition to the dislocation allowance, the temporary lodging allowance, or the advance station housing allowance.

Other circumstances can occur where you are "caught short of funds" that are essential to the proper performance of your duty. For instance, if a uniform is damaged and must be replaced, you are expected to pay for the replacement based on the clothing allowance you have been receiving. Under emergency conditions, if you are without funds to purchase the needed clothing items, you can charge them. This debt must also be repaid, and generally it is deducted in full from your next month's pay. If a one-time collection would cause you undue financial hardship, however, you may request a monthly collection plan with payments at least as large as the monthly clothing allowance.

DEDUCTIONS FROM YOUR PAY

The LES reflects many types of deductions made from your pay, some voluntary or optional deductions and other required deductions such as taxes.

Federal income taxes are collected based on your taxable pay. Most allowances are not taxable. Federal Insurance Contributions Act (FICA) charges are also required from all soldiers.

State income taxes are not collected from all soldiers. Every soldier has a Home of Record that establishes the rules the FAO uses in computing any necessary state income tax withholdings. Some states, for instance, charge no state income tax to soldiers who are legal residents of that state but are stationed elsewhere; other states never require state income taxes from the soldier on active duty. The latter category includes Alaska, Florida, Illinois, Michigan, Montana, Nevada, New Hampshire, South Dakota, Tennessee, Texas, Vermont, Washington, Wyoming, and foreign or U.S. territories.

Another required deduction is the involuntary contribution each soldier makes to the United States Soldier's Home (USSH). This monthly deduction is small, however (50 cents a month as of January 1986).

Servicemen's Group Life Insurance (SGLI) is an option, although most soldiers elect to take this inexpensive term life insurance policy. The maximum allowable insurance is $50,000. While the insurance coverage is optional, the deduction is automatically made (and the insurance automatically provided) unless the soldier specifically requests no coverage or reduced coverage, through the local FAO. The rate for the insurance is 8 cents per month per $1,000 coverage; this means the maximum insurance of $50,000 costs the soldier $4 per month.

Involuntary deductions from your pay can also be made as a result of court-martial sentencing or nonjudicial punishment; repayment of your indebtedness to the Army; collection of back taxes; collection of overpayment due to administrative error; enforcement of child support or alimony obligations when ordered by the civilian courts; or collection of dishonored checks written to the commissary or other military store, if the check has not been honored within seven days after you are notified of the returned check.

Under special circumstances your indebtedness to the Army can be cancelled or remitted. Handled on a case-by-case basis through your com-

mander, cancellation or remission of indebtedness is not commonplace—
but you should be aware that under extreme circumstances, it is possible.

Voluntary deductions from your pay cover a wide variety of choices.
Educational contribution programs, where the military adds funds to contributions you make toward your future educational benefits, are a matter
of choice (covered in detail in chapter 3). These voluntary deductions
would be shown on the monthly LES.

Another voluntary deduction is made when you elect to use government laundry and drycleaning services through your unit. The charges for
these services are deducted automatically each month until you request
termination of the service or upon your PCS.

Allotments are another form of voluntary deductions. Many different
kinds of allotments are recognized, but DA Form 3684 can generally be
used to initiate the allotment.

AER allotments are used to repay loans from the Army Emergency
Relief fund. This allotment will not be established for less than three
months or for less than $5 per month. AER-C allotments are used to make
voluntary contributions to the AER fund. The term of the AER-C is limited
to not less than three months but no more than twelve months, for no less
than $1 per month.

CFC allotments, similar to the AER-C, is a voluntary contribution for
the purpose of paying pledges to the Combined Federal Campaign fund.
CFC allotments are always 12 months long, January to December, for no
less than $2 per month.

SPT-V allotments allow you to make voluntary contributions to your
family, divorced spouse, or dependent relative, through a bank, building
and loan association, or credit union, to the individual's account. Such
allotments can also be made directly to the allotee. While you can have
multiple SPT-V allotments, not more than one can be made to any allotee.
If the allotment is made to an institution, you are responsible for making
any necessary arrangements for proper crediting.

FININ allotments are made to financial organizations for credit to
your savings, checking, or trust accounts. These moneys may be used for
any purpose you direct, including repayment of loans made by the financial institution. You may have only two such allotments.

HOME allotments are made for the purpose of paying a mortgage on a
home, mobile home, or house trailer that you use as a residence. Only one
such allotment is authorized.

INS allotments are used to make premiums on commercial life insurance policies. Such allotments cannot be used for premiums on policies
covering your spouse or children, or for health, accident, or hospitalization insurance. Multiple INS allotments are authorized.

Bond allotments allow you to purchase U.S. Savings Bonds through payroll deductions. The allotment covers the full charge for the bond. The bonds can be mailed to you, the owner, the co-owner, or the beneficiary, or can be retained at the U.S. Army Finance and Accounting Center for safekeeping. Multiple allotments are allowed.

MBOND allotments give you flexibility in purchasing U.S. Savings Bonds, because the purchase can cover a period of two to four months. Multiple MBOND allotments are authorized, and mailing bonds follow the same rules as above.

REDCR allotments are used to repay loans made from the American Red Cross. Multiple allotments are allowed, but must extend for at least three months and are made for not less than $5 a month.

EDSAV allotments cover voluntary contributions made to your Veterans Educational Assistance Program (VEAP). Only one allotment can be made, ranging from $25 to $100 per month.

8

The Obvious and Not So Obvious

Every soldier who has ever served in the Army is aware that the military lifestyle differs from the civilian community. The esprit de corps, the team effort, and the shared hardships combine to mold a unique community.

The Army community offers you and your family a myriad of "extras" that could be easily missed by a first-termer if someone didn't point them out. Post orientations are intended to do just that—point out the "hidden benefits" of the Army lifestyle.

Some are not hidden. What soldier could miss the Post Exchange or movie theater? The post gymnasium is another popular attraction on Army posts throughout the world. The bowling alleys and clubs also boast a busy nightlife. Military families learn quickly where the commissary and child care facilities are on post.

Other services deserve a bit of highlighting. Even the obvious services may have hidden wrinkles you have not considered. For instance, soldiers living in the barracks frequently avoid shopping at the commissary because they are only picking up a few things. With savings ranging from 20 to 35 percent over civilian grocery stores, however, even a short list would produce a sizable savings. In addition, commissaries provide quick checkout service for those individuals purchasing ten items or less. Most commissaries also give priority to serving the soldier during the lunch hour: if in uniform, you can go to the front of the line in many commissaries.

Many PXs offer catalog shopping now in addition to the department-store exchange. Credit cards are now accepted in exchanges, as well. In addition, the PX offers a very liberal layaway plan especially for large purchases. This allows you to spread the payments over three to six months for a nominal fee.

RELIEF AGENCIES: HELP'S AVAILABLE

Financial emergencies can sometimes arise in your life, and it is at those times the expression "the Army takes care of its own" has a special meaning. Through Army Emergency Relief (AER) assistance, Army personnel and their families, reservists on active duty, and needy widows and orphans of deceased Army members, can receive help for a myriad of problems.

Conducted in coordination with the American Red Cross, AER is a private nonprofit corporation that serves as the Army's emergency financial assistance organization. It provides emergency loans to eligible recipients who are faced with unforeseen, urgent situations requiring immediate financial attention. Under special circumstances, grants (requiring no repayment) may also be provided. Most assistance, however, is through loans.

Any soldier facing a *real* emergency should be provided AER assistance, but assistance is not provided when the request is based on convenience or comfort instead of valid need. Examples of authorized emergencies include nonreceipt of pay, allowances, or allotments; loss of funds due to theft; authorized medical care under CHAMPUS that requires a down payment; funeral expenses incurred for a dependent or parent; travel expenses needed for emergency leave; payment of initial rent and deposit, or payment of rent to avoid eviction; payment of utility bills to avoid termination of utility services; cost of vehicle repairs when required for safe operation; cost of vehicle insurance premiums; and privately owned vehicle deemed essential because transportation is needed for an ill dependent or pregnant wife.

Except for unusual circumstances, AER assistance is not authorized for divorces, marriages, ordinary leave or vacations, consolidation of debts, business ventures or investments, legal fees, income taxes, continuing assistance, gambling debts, or funds to replace those overdrawn from bank accounts.

Loan repayments generally begin on the first day of the second month after the assistance is provided. For example, for a loan made in the middle of January the first payment would be due March 1, and would be made by allotment from the end of February pay. Loan payments can be spread out over a 12-month period, or until the individual's expiration of term of service (ETS)—whichever period is *shorter*.

The American Red Cross provides another form of help—that of verifying the emergency so that the commander can act more swiftly to help the soldier. This is especially the case when the soldier is assigned overseas and an emergency occurs elsewhere, often literally halfway around the world. The first details of a family emergency are frequently sketchy at best, and confusing at their worst. The Red Cross works on behalf of the soldier to gather the facts and provide him with clear information so an appropriate decision or action can be made. The role of the Red Cross is intricately involved with command decisions on emergency leave and compassionate reassignments, deferments, or hardship discharges.

The Army Community Service Center provides a different but vital type of assistance. Counselors there provide referral services to the military family and to the soldier, as well as in-house counseling on such matters as budgeting, personal or family problems, community services available in the civilian community (libraries, parks and recreations programs, and so on), special educational needs for gifted or handicapped children, and assistance for the military spouse seeking employment in a new community. In addition, almost all ACS centers maintain a lending closet with items such as bedding, dishes, and other household goods that may be needed before PCS shipment arrives. Larger installations often have 24-hour hotlines through ACS to help with late-night emergencies.

A HOME AWAY FROM HOME—THE USO

The USO is a frequently overlooked military benefit. With PCS moves an accepted part of military life, the USO provides a haven for the newcomer—a place to have a cup of coffee, meet some of the local citizens, relax and have a small slice of "Americana" no matter where you are assigned.

USOs often feature name entertainers. In addition they provide cultural exchanges, local tours, socials, dances, recreation halls, free movies, and a relaxing atmosphere where you can just "get away from it all" for awhile.

In large metropolitan areas in CONUS, USOs are also available. Many large airports have a small USO facility for military travelers.

SPECIAL SERVICES

Most soldiers are familiar with the gymnasium, one of the many facilities run by special services. But on many posts much, much more is available. Special Services frequently rents camping gear, tents, trailers, boats and trailers, and other items at affordable prices. Some installations charge by rank—the more you have, the more you pay.

Tours are another benefit offered by Special Services. Group travel can bring costs into a more manageable range, and Special Services provides guides for all group tours they sponsor.

TRAVEL BENEFITS—AT A PRICE THAT CAN'T BE BEAT

Space-available travel, often called "Space-A," is a means by which you (and your family) can catch a free ride on a government plane that happens to be going in the right direction. No travel agents help out here though, and reservations are not allowed. In fact, as the name implies, soldiers fly for free if there is extra room not needed by cargo or by personnel on government business.

The process is not complicated. You sign in on a register and then wait. Priorities are established through a full set of regulations. Top priority goes to the soldier on emergency leave.

Servicemembers must be on leave to use Space-A flights. Soldiers cannot get around the waiting period—which can be extensive—by signing up for a flight and then reporting back to duty for the interim wait. Attempting such a trick usually means the soldier is charged for annual leave even though he returned to duty for several days.

To use the free service, the soldier simply must be prepared to "wait-it-out." A one-time-per-trip administration fee of $10 is charged. Luggage is strictly limited to two bags and a total maximum weight of 66 pounds.

LEGAL ASSISTANCE

Legal services available to the soldier are one of those hidden extras that can be easily overlooked. Yet the services the legal office can provide are significant.

First, the legal officer can help you understand the military justice system. You have certain well-defined rights under the military system of law. Among these, the most basic are the right to due process of law, the right to a defense lawyer, the right to remain silent, and certain rights under search and seizure.

Due process has the same meaning in the military environment as it does in the civilian legal system: a person must be considered innocent until proven guilty. Guilt can be determined only through trial where evidence is presented. The defendant cannot be found guilty unless the government proves beyond a reasonable doubt that he did indeed commit the offense. The soldier has the right to be present to hear and cross-examine all witnesses. He can call witnesses for the defense and present evidence, as well. Often these functions are performed on behalf of the soldier by a defense lawyer, assigned free of charge, from the Judge Advocate General's (JAG) Corps.

JAG lawyers are fully qualified attorneys who have the same obligations to their clients as a civilian attorney. The lawyer acts in the best interest of the client—and cannot reveal anything the soldier says under the attorney-client relationship. Soldiers always have the right to free counsel when facing a special court-martial or a general court-martial; sometimes free counsel will be provided when the soldier faces a summary court-martial, although this is not always required under the military justice system. Under any circumstances, the soldier has the right to acquire a civilian lawyer of his choosing, but the cost of such services must be paid by the defendant.

Whatever the legal proceedings, the soldier has the right to remain silent. No soldier is required to provide information that may be incriminating. As in the civilian environment, the accused must be advised of his right to remain silent before being questioned. If the soldier was not so advised, any testimony obtained through that questioning cannot be used in a court-martial against the accused.

The rights under search and seizure are quite different for the soldier and the civilian. While still protected by the Fourth Amendment to the Constitution of the United States, the soldier can have his person or property searched under certain circumstances. For instance, the commanding officer can order a search of any soldier under his command. This search can also be carried out for any soldier's property. The order for a search, however, must be based on probable cause.

When a soldier is apprehended (arrested), he is subject to a legal search. Any personal property in the immediate possession of the soldier at the time of arrest can also be searched. If a soldier agrees to a search, the search is legal. Perhaps the most significant difference between the civilian's and soldier's search rights is that the soldier's person or property may be legally searched under an inspection to check unit readiness. Criminal evidence found during a unit inspection is therefore admissable at a military trial.

Minor offenses are often handled by administrative measures through the Article 15, a nonjudicial punishment under the United Code of Military Justice (UCMJ). The soldier must be notified in writing that the commanding officer plans to impose an Article 15. If, however, the soldier requests an open hearing, he can choose trial by court-martial. Generally the soldier has 72 hours to decide which type of hearing he prefers, and has the right to discuss such a decision with a lawyer. It should be noted that punishment under a court-martial can be more severe.

A commanding officer who imposes an Article 15 also has clemency powers: the power to lessen a punishment, suspend punishment, or remit or cancel any parts of the punishment not yet served. Clemency is based on the commander's feelings that the soldier is deserving due to past performance.

Every soldier has the right to appeal an Article 15. Reasons for appeal include nonguilt, unduly severe punishment, or failure by the commander to follow the rules for giving the Article 15. Such appeals are made to the commander immediately above the commander who gave the Article 15, and should be made within 15 days.

All legal problems do not involve criminal action. Many types of assistance are routinely provided through the JAG Office. Documents such as powers of attorney and wills can be handled through a military lawyer. In addition, advice on the legal aspects of marriage, divorce, debts, adoption, child support, taxes, claims against the government, motor vehicle registration, or change of name can be attained through the military legal system. Appeals of an Enlisted Evaluation Report can also be initiated through the JAG Office.

The Soldiers' and Sailors' Civil Relief Act (SSCRA) is a federal law that helps soldiers who have difficulty meeting their legal obligations because they are in the military service. Under the Act, a soldier who incurred debts before joining the Army may be able to reduce the amount of the monthly payment, but the debts themselves will not be forgiven. In addition, the Act can protect a soldier who is sued through a court located far from where the soldier is stationed. Again, the legal suit is not dismissed but only postponed until the soldier can attend the court. It should be noted that the Act does not protect a soldier from a lease he signs after joining the Army. Military transfer does not automatically cancel a lease.

Complaints can also be handled through the legal office when the soldier feels his complaint should be handled by someone other than the First Sergeant or commanding officer. The Inspector General (IG) receives complaints, investigates the facts, and turns the case over to the official who can best correct the situation if indeed the complaint is justified. If the IG finds that the soldier registering the complaint did not have all the facts, the IG will try to explain the reasons for the situation to the soldier.

If a complaint cannot be solved at the local level, it is referred to the next higher command and ultimately can be referred to the Inspector General of the Army. Soldiers may make complaints when they feel they have been wronged by a commanding officer, when they feel a civilian business has discriminated against them, or when they feel a situation needs correcting. Many complaints, however, can be handled at the company level.

Legal restrictions exist for every soldier. Soldiers may not accept gifts or solicit contributions for gifts from other soldiers who are junior in grade or rank. In addition, a soldier may not sell goods or services to another soldier junior in grade or rank. Exceptions are made when a soldier sells personal property or a home on a one-time basis to another soldier. A soldier's freedom of expression also is more restricted than that of a civilian. For example, a soldier cannot speak out in public against civilian leaders, campaign for a political candidate, or attend a demonstration while wearing a military uniform. In addition, soldiers should not use military rank or title when writing a letter to an editor.

9

Career Decisions

More than half the soldiers who first enlist in the Army do not make the military a career choice. They serve one enlistment, or maybe more, and return to civilian life to pursue other goals. They carry with them a wealth of experience, however, such as formal military or civilian training, and many memories.

Others decide that the Army is where they belong. They may have found their niche on the first enlistment and may be ready to pursue a career in that MOS. On the other hand, they may decide to stay with the Army but might still be searching for just the right spot within the Army's vast system.

In any case, as the ETS date approaches, the soldier is at a crossroads. Many different paths lead from the present, but only one can be taken into the future. The choice is crucial because life tomorrow is built on the foundation laid today. Information about the many possibilities in the Army may clarify the issues for you.

DISCHARGES

Several types of discharges exist for the soldier who has decided to leave the military. By far the most desirable is the Honorable Discharge. (Incidently, it is by far the most common, as well.) A soldier can be denied an honorable discharge only on the basis of a pattern of misbehavior, and not on an isolated instance. A General Discharge is reserved for the soldier whose service to the Army has been satisfactory, but not meritorious.

Many other types of discharges exist. The Discharge at the Convenience of the Army can be either an Honorable or a General Discharge, depending on the soldier's conduct while he was on active duty.

Dependency or Hardship Discharges are used when a soldier's continued service would put his family in serious dependency or hardship. The dependency can be based on the death or disability of the soldier's family or his spouse's family; it can be based on the sole surviving son or daughter of a family; or it can be based on the role of sole parent.

PREGNANCY: THE SOLDIER'S OPTIONS

Career decisions abound for the young soldier—whether the military should be a full career or a stepping-stone to a civilian career; what training to seek; which geographic preferences to select; and how best to enhance his military professionalism and promotion potential. The soldier who then discovers she is pregnant is faced with another complete set of choices.

The most basic decision a pregnant soldier must make is whether to continue in the military. She may choose at that time to separate from the Army or to stay in the Service. This decision can be a difficult one to make because of its far-reaching ramifications. Once the soldier has decided to be retained on active duty, she will be expected to complete her full enlistment before she is again given the choice of continuing in the military or returning to civilian life.

"Staying In"

Staying in the military as a mother of a newborn child does not afford the soldier "special privileges." The soldier normally will not receive PCS orders for an overseas assignment during the pregnancy, and such orders can often be deferred or deleted if they should indeed be issued. (See the section on *overseas Assignments* in chapter 5 for more details.) After the child is born and the mother is released from normal postnatal care, however, the military mother is given no unique consideration for assignments. She is expected to fulfill the needs of the Army just like any other soldier. This means that she could receive orders for worldwide assignments, including to dependent-restricted overseas assignments.

The Army is concerned for the welfare of the child, but it does not adjust the assignment process to accommodate the new mother. Instead, the Army requires each soldier with minor dependents to file an approved Family Care Plan. Failure to complete an adequate plan will result in a bar to reenlistment. The plan specifies what actions the soldier has taken to ensure care for her dependents in the event she is assigned to an area where dependents are not authorized. In addition, she is expected to make provisions for the care for her dependents while she is away from her home for military duty (on a daily basis and in the event of a necessary TDY).

The Family Care Plan is not required of only the pregnant soldier; it is also required of all enlisted personnel in grade E5 and under, who have dependents who would not be able to take care of themselves in the case of the absence of the soldier.

One other consequence of the pregnant soldier's decision to continue in the military is the possibility of involuntary separation. If the soldier cannot handle her normal duties during the pregnancy or once she is a new mother, she may be separated from the service involuntarily. Such decisions are made on the grounds of unsatisfactory performance of duty or misconduct, whichever is appropriate. Separation involuntarily is covered by AR 635-200, Paragraphs 5-8 and 13-2, in addition to Chapters 11 and 14.

The pregnant soldier will be provided medical care during and after the pregnancy. Again, she has a choice. She may remain at her present duty assignment and receive care through a military facility within 30 miles of that location; or if such care is not available, she will be treated through a civilian doctor and civilian facilities. On the other hand, she may choose to take ordinary leave, advance leave, and excess leave so that she may return to her home or other appropriate and desired location for her maternity care and the birth of her child.

Once labor begins, her leave status will change to convalescent leave for the period of labor, hospitalization, and postpartum care. Convalescent leave for postpartum care is limited to the amount of time the doctor specifies as essential for the medical needs of the mother. Leave status and the pregnant soldier are covered in AR 630-5, Chapter 9, Section II.

If the soldier decides to return to her home for the purpose of delivering the baby, it is her responsibility to first ensure that military facilities near her home have obstetrical care available; many military hospitals do not provide such care. The soldier cannot choose to return home for maternity care and have the government pay for that care at a civilian facility. This is prohibited in AR 40-3, except for bona fide medical emergencies that justify the use of a civilian facility. Using civilian facilities away from the duty location means that the soldier, not the government, is normally responsible for the medical bills. The Health Benefits Counselor at the nearest military medical facility is the best source for further information on this matter.

The Army provides maternity uniforms at no cost to the soldier who decides to continue her military career after she learns she is pregnant. In addition, BAQ or government quarters will be provided under standard military guidelines, depending on the availability of quarters at the installation where the new mother is assigned. The Post Housing Office at each installation and the First Sergeant at each unit are good sources for more details.

Separating from Service

The pregnant soldier can choose to separate from the Army. She would receive an honorable discharge and any benefits applicable to soldiers with the amount of time in service that she would have at the time of separation.

Medical treatment for obstetrical and postpartum care would be provided at goverment expense *through a military medical facility*. The separating soldier could not use CHAMPUS or civilian medical facilities at government expense. In fact, the pregnant soldier is required to sign a statement before she decides to separate from the military, clearly stating that she understands that under no circumstance can CHAMPUS, any military department, or the Veterans Administration reimburse her civilian maternity care expenses; the statement further clarifies that she understands that any costs for civilian care will be her personal financial responsibility. Therefore, careful planning must be made to ensure that she settles in an area where military medical facilities provide maternity care. The separating pregnant soldier will be authorized postpartum care for up to six weeks after the birth of the child.

Help is Available

The decision to stay in or separate from the Army will never be an easy decision to make. Recognizing this, the Army provides a counselor for each pregnant soldier to ensure that she understands her options. In addition, a great deal of additional help is available. The Chaplain's Service can provide counseling; the JAG Office can instruct the soldier in legal matters regarding the upcoming birth and care of her child; the American Red Cross can provide another source of counseling; and the First Sergeant can help the soldier assess the impact on her career.

THE REENLISTMENT BONUS

A special program has been developed by the Army in an effort to increase the number of soldiers reenlisting or extending in certain MOSs. These occupational specialties are considered critical MOSs, and are determined by inadequate retention or reenlistment levels. It is impossible to list the critical MOSs since the list is not constant; the Army updates its list on a regular basis and publishes it through the DA Circular 611 series. The unit's First Sergeant should be able to provide the list to interested soldiers.

The Selective Reenlistment Bonus (SRB) Program is available to all soldiers, regardless of rank, who hold a primary MOS designated as critical. Soldiers reenlisting through the SRB Program are eligible for reenlistment bonuses of up to $20,000 if they reenlist or extend for a minimum of 3 years. They may receive a maximum of three such SRBs during their military career, and only one in each established time zone. The zones, based on time of active military service, are: Zone A, extending from 21 months to 6 years; Zone B, from 6 to 10 years; and Zone C, from 10 to 14 years of active military service.

The actual amount of the SRB is determined by a formula based on the soldier's monthly basic pay. The bonus cannot exceed six times the monthly pay, multiplied by the number of years of additional obligated service, nor can the bonus exceed a maximum of $20,000. The SRB is based on the current needs of the Army and on current reenlistment trends in specific MOSs. The more critical the Army's need, the higher the SRB. Consequently, frequently no MOS qualified for the maximum rate allowable. For instance, as of 31 January 1986, soldiers in 118 MOSs could receive SRBs, but the highest rate available for any MOS at that time was four times the monthly basic pay, times the number of years of additional obligation. In addition, the January 1986 list limited SRBs to soldiers only in Zone A and Zone B.

The following examples illustrate how the program operates. A soldier receiving basic pay of $800 a month reenlists under the SRB Program for 4 years; the bonus amount for his MOS is the maximum, six times the monthly basic pay. The SRB bonus would be [$800 x 6] x 4 = $19,200. If, however, the soldier was receiving a basic pay of $1,000 a month, the SRB bonus would not be [$1,000 x 6] x 4 = $24,000; instead, this soldier would receive the maximum allowable bonus—$20,000. Another soldier is receiving the basic pay of $800 a month, but is in an MOS for which the

Army only pays two times the monthly pay. That soldier, reenlisting for 4 years, would receive [$800 x 2] x 4 = $6,400.

Since qualifying MOSs and their SRB rates fluctuate based on the needs of the Army, interested soldiers should contact their respective First Sergeants to obtain the most current information.

The SRB bonus will be paid in addition to any other pay and allowance to which the soldier is already entitled.

THE ARMY RESERVE

Another option for the decision-making soldier is the Army Reserve. This wholly federal military force is composed of the Ready Reserve and the Standby Reserve. The Ready Reserve is made up of combat support and combat service support units, available for quick mobilization in times of national emergency or war. The Standby Reserve, on the other hand, is a pool of soldiers who have a remaining military obligation and are eligible for recall to active duty.

Through the Ready Reserve, the former soldier can supplement his civilian income while taking full advantage of the leadership training he received while on active duty. Reservists receive four days pay for each weekend of Reserve training, usually held monthly. An additional requirement is a two-week annual training. Salary ranges depend on time in service and pay grade. For instance, an E5 reservist with four years' time in service would receive $2,085 annually.

If a soldier leaving active duty enlists in the Ready Reserve within 60 days of discharge from the Army, he retains the same active Army rank, pay grade, and time in grade. Privileges include the $50,000 SGLI, space available dental care, and commissary and post exchange privileges (one shopping day for each four hours of Reserve training).

All Army installations have a Reenlistment NCO who can provide more detailed information.

THE ARMY NATIONAL GUARD

The Army National Guard is a dual federal-state military force, with the primary mission of maintaining combat divisions and support units available for active duty in time of national emergency or war. Under its state mission, the Guard protects life and property and preserves state internal security.

Pay and benefits are essentially the same for the Guard as for the Reserve. One unique feature about the Guard is their OCS program. The one-year program provides all training on the weekend format through the state OCS; Guard members can also attend the active Army OCS and earn a commission in 14 weeks.

The Reenlistment NCO can provide information on the National Guard programs, as well.

ACTIVE DUTY IN ANOTHER CAPACITY

The decision-making soldier may also elect to remain on active duty. Choices still abound, however. Upon reenlistment the soldier can elect additional training, a particular duty station elsewhere, or current duty station stabilization.

Possible training options for the first-termer include airborne training, U.S. Army Intelligence and Security Command and Electronic Warfare training, U.S. Army Information Systems Command training, Language School training, and other MOSs that have openings for new soldiers who qualify. Other options include reenlisting for Special Forces, combat arms unit of choice, the U.S. Army Berlin Brigade, and the U.S. Army 3d Infantry (Old Guard).

Soldiers willing to extend their enlistment or reenlist can apply for a number of interesting career development programs: Explosive Ordnance Disposal, Enlisted Club Management, Presidential Support Activities (working at the White House), Technical Escort (for chemical, ammunitions, and EOD specialists), Army Bands, instructors at service schools, drill sergeants, and recruiters. Information and requirements for each career program are contained in AR 614-200; Reenlistment NCOs can also be of assistance to the soldier who wishes to explore some of the more unusual career options within the Army system.

Officer Candidate School (OCS)

Enlisted personnel who elect to remain on active duty can apply for Officer Candidate School training. Age restrictions require that the prospective student be between 19.5 and 29 years old upon enrollment in the program. In addition, candidates must have a minimum of two years of college training and at least a 90 on the officer selection battery (OSB).

Regardless of rank at the time of acceptance to OCS, students are paid at the E5 level during the 14 weeks of training. OCS graduates are commissioned as Second Lieutenants (O1).

Warrant Officer Flight Training (WOFT)

Helicopter pilot training is provided through the Warrant Officer

Special Forces: Rappelling

Flight Training program. Applicants for this program are required to be high school graduates, have a score of 90 or above on the revised Flight Aptitude Selection Test, have a GT score of at least 110, and pass the Class 1 Flight Physical Examination at Fort Rucker. The flight physical must be less than one year old at the time the student reports to the training program. Soldiers incur a four-year service obligation from the date of graduation as a Warrant Officer.

Reenlistment NCOs can provide further details and necessary forms for WOFT.

A Road to the U.S. Military Academy at West Point

The pinnacle of military education, in the opinion of many, would have to be the U.S. Military Academy at West Point. In the spirit of "the Army taking care of its own," special provisions have been made to aid enlisted soldiers who may wish to strive toward the goal of gaining admission to the Academy. The United States Military Academy Preparatory School (USMAPS) provides a path of upward mobility for enlisted men and women. The sole function of the Preparatory School is to mold its students into qualified West Point cadets. Its success rate is impressive— approximately 95 percent of its graduates gain admission to West Point.

With so much to gain through the program, the soldier might expect to pay a high price for the opportunity. However, the only price he would pay would be in the dedication and perseverance that would be expected of any serious student. The soldier continues to receive full pay and benefits, is provided housing and meals, and is still eligible for promotions under standard Department of Army policies. There are no tuition or fees to be paid. In fact, the only expense a soldier incurs is about $300 worth of distinctive clothing and school supplies. What is more surprising is that the soldier incurs no additional service obligation by attending the Preparatory School.

Located at Fort Monmouth, New Jersey, USMAPS provides academic, military, and physical training. The ten-month school, divided into two semesters, emphasizes English and mathematics in the academic arena. The August-to-January term helps prepare students for the Scholastic Aptitude Tests (SAT) and American College Test (ACT). SAT and ACT scores are required for admission to most colleges and universities. The small class size and individual attention aid students in mastering algebra, plane geometry, trigonometry, and introductory work in analytic geometry and calculus. English courses emphasize grammar, usage, rhetoric, reading comprehension, vocabulary development, literature, and composition.

Two daily required study sessions help students stay abreast of their studies.

Military training is part of the daily routine as well. No soldier retains his "official rank" while at the school. All are considered "cadet candidates" and are addressed as "Mister" or "Miss." Throughout the program, cadet candidates rotate among various leadership positions in the cadet battalion so that each has the opportunity to develop leadership potential.

Physical training is another highlight of USMAPS. In preparation for the rigors of cadet life at West Point, cadet candidates participate in physical education and intramural sports on a daily basis, developing their strength, coordination, and stamina. As an option, students may choose among a variety of school teams that compete with community colleges, other preparatory schools, and junior varsity college teams in the area. Teams include football, soccer, cross country, volleyball, men's and women's basketball, wrestling, indoor and outdoor track, baseball, lacrosse, tennis, swimming, softball, golf, and orienteering.

Dances, pep rallies, clubs, student government, and yearbook and newspaper staffs are but a few of the extracurricular and social functions that round out the collegiate atmosphere of the Preparatory School. Leaves and passes are offered as privileges for weekends, holidays, and semester breaks. Visits by friends or family during the school week are discouraged, however, due to the students' heavy school commitment.

To qualify for admission, soldiers must be:

- A United States citizen.
- At least 17 but not yet 21 years old on July 1 of the year entering the school.
- Not married and without dependents.
- Physically qualified (pregnancy is a disqualifying factor).
- A high school graduate (or the equivalent).
- Of high moral character.

To apply, soldiers must submit a complete application package no later than March 15 of the year in which they hope to enter the school. The packet consists of:

- A letter of application.
- A legible copy of the most recent Medical Examination (SF 88) and Report of Medical History (SF 93), neither more than one year old.
- A complete high school transcript, or a copy of the GED certificate with test scores.
- College transcripts for any college credit received.

- GT score.
- ETS date (The soldier must have enough time in service remaining to complete the school; if not, he must extend or reenlist before arriving at the school.)
- Most recent Army Physical Fitness Test score, not more than one year old.
- Results of SAT.
- A recent photograph.
- An evaluation by his immediate commanding officer.
- A handwritten, one-page essay on the questions—"Why I Wish to Attend USMAPS" and "What Are My Goals In Life."

Further information can be obtained by contacting:

Admissions
USMAPS
Fort Monmouth, NJ 07703-5509

Phone: (201) 532-1807
Autovon: 992-1807

ROTC

One other option for the soldier is to separate from the service under a special ROTC scholarship program, earn a degree, be commissioned a second lieutenant, and return to active duty.

College study part-time can mean a long road before the goal of a baccalaureate degree is reached. Determination and persistence are essential traveling tools if the final destination is to be achieved. But the Army has provided a way for 200 soldiers annually to be discharged from the service early to attend college full-time under the Army ROTC Program.

The Army Reserve Officers' Training Corps (ROTC) offers two- and three-year scholarships for active duty enlisted personnel. These soldiers become civilians specifically to enter the ROTC program, complete the baccalaureate program, and then be commissioned as officers in the Regular Army or the U.S. Army Reserve. Once discharged, the soldier forfeits the pay and benefits of active duty, but he may still use any veterans educational benefits earned while on active duty. In addition a monthly stipend of $100 is provided, as well as full payment of college tuition, fees, and standard allowance for books and college supplies.

The ROTC cadet is not a soldier in civilian clothes. The former soldier

Obstacle Course

leads the life of a normal college student with very few additional responsibilities. Cadets must complete prescribed military science courses, a minimum of one semester of foreign language, an ROTC Advanced Camp (a paid six-week training program between the junior and senior years), and any other training required by the Secretary of the Army as a requirement for commissioning.

Returning to active duty as a Regular Army second lieutenant is not a guarantee. Based on the needs of the Army, some cadets are commissioned as second lieutenants in the U.S. Army Reserves instead. Cadets select the branch of service in which they would prefer to serve, but branch selection is also not guaranteed; again, the needs of the Army must take precedence. Active duty service can sometimes be delayed up to two years at the request of the individual in order to complete postgraduate studies; educational delays are also based on the needs of the Army at the time of commissioning.

How can a soldier be counted among the 200 scholarship recipients? First, he must have completed at least one year of college but not more than two years of college; 125 soldiers will be selected for the three-year scholarships and 75 others will be selected for the two-year scholarships. Scholarships cover the *time remaining to finish the degree*. To be eligible, the soldier must:

- Be a citizen of the United States.
- Be on active duty at least until June 1 of the year in which he will begin full-time college study in September.
- Be less than 25 years of age on June 30 of the year in which he will receive a commission. (This requirement can be adjusted up to four years based on time spent on active duty. For instance, a soldier with two years' active duty service would have to be younger than 27 on June 30 of the year of commissioning.)
- Be medically qualified. (Medical qualifications for ROTC are more stringent than those for general active duty service.)
- Demonstrate strong leadership potential.
- Have a General Technical (GT) Aptitude Area score of at least 115 from the Army Classification Battery of tests administered before induction into the Army.
- Have an accumulative grade point average of 2.0 on a 4.0 scale for all college work completed thus far.
- Have passed the Army Physical Fitness Test within the past year with a minimum score of 180 and a minimum of 60 points in each event.
- Be accepted as an academic junior for the two-year scholarship, or

as an academic sophomore for the three-year scholarship, by an institution offering Army ROTC.

If a servicemember has a bar to reenlistment, plans on studying for the ministry, has completed one undergraduate degree and is working on a second, or is in the weight control program, he is ineligible for the scholarship program.

It should be noted that in 1985 some of the available scholarships went unawarded simply because not enough soldiers applied. Putting in an application is not "a long shot."

Soldiers may apply to the program between December 15 (of the preceding year) and March 31 of the year in which they wish to enroll in school. Applications, available as early as October 15, should be submitted early in this period so that any missing information or documents can be supplied *before the April 1 deadline*. Incomplete packets, as of April, will not be considered. The application packet can be requested from:

> U.S. Army ROTC Cadet Command
> ATTN: ATCC-C
> Fort Monroe, VA 23651-5000

Packets consist of several forms:

- TRADOC Form 471-1-R, Application for Active Duty Enlisted Personnel 2- and 3-Year ROTC Scholarship. The soldier completes this form.
- TRADOC Form 471-2-R, Active Duty Enlisted Personnel 2- and 3-Year ROTC Scholarship Application Data. The soldier gives this form to his immediate supervisor, who evaluates the soldier's performance and potential. The form is then routed to the supervisor's commander, and higher up the chain of command if that individual is not a field grade officer.
- TRADOC Form 113-R (ROTC Scholarship Applicant Snapshot). A full-length photo is preferred; one in military uniform is desirable.
- TRADOC Form 477-R-FL (Letter of Acceptance). This form must be completed by the university or college the soldier wishes to attend. Soldiers must complete university enrollment application forms and be accepted by the university *before* school officials can complete this form. Separate application forms may be required for the school's ROTC program; the Professor of Military Science must also complete part of Form 477-R-FL.

Transcripts from all colleges where the soldier has received academic credit are also required before the April 1 deadline. Additionally, official test results must be furnished for any college credit obtained through CLEP or USAFI.

Soldiers accepted into the program will be assigned an early discharge date prior to the beginning of the school program. At their discharge, they will enlist for eight years in the U.S. Army Reserve. School time counts toward the Reserve obligation. Upon graduation from college, all scholarship recipients apply for an Army commission. Those receiving a Reserve commission finish their obligation in a local Reserve unit. Those receiving a Regular Army commission return to active duty. If they later terminate their Army career *before* the original eight-year obligation has expired, they must finish the remaining obligation with the Reserves.

Some limitations are placed on what a scholarship recipient may study. The Army needs highly trained, technical officers, so the preponderance of scholarships go to enlisted soldiers planning on entering technical fields. Six categories have been established. Percentages of total recipients for the 1986–87 school year were as follows:

Engineering	30%
Physical Science	25%
Business	20%
Social Sciences	10%
Nursing	7%
Other	8%

"Other" can include humanities, medical fields, or pre-law.

For the soldier interested in a possible career as an Army officer, or the soldier who simply wants to shorten his road toward the baccalaureate degree, the ROTC Scholarship Program offers a viable alternative.

CONCLUSION

No simple conclusion can be drawn. The choices abound for the first-termer. The impact of the choices is tremendous, because today's decisions create your future.

Information is the best weapon you can have when faced with life-changing decisions. It is for that specific purpose that this chapter was included.

The decisions are yours. Consider the options well before attempting to reach a conclusion.

Glossary

Selected Acronyms and Abbreviations

ACES	Army Continuing Education System
ACS	Army Community Service
ADAPC	Army Alcohol and Drug Abuse Prevention and Control Program
AEA	Assignment eligibility and availability
AER	Army Emergency Relief
AFQT	Armed Forces Qualification Test
AI	Assignment instruction
AIT	Advanced individual training
AMOS	Additional military occupational specialty
ANCOC	Advanced Noncommissioned Officers Course
APOD	Aerial port of debarkation
APOE	Aerial port of embarkation
APRT	Army Physical Readiness Test
AR	Army regulation
ARC	American Red Cross
ASEP	Advanced Skills Education Program

ASI	Additional skill identifier
AWOL	Absent without leave
BASD	Basic active service date
BDU	Battle dress uniform
BESD	Basic enlisted service date
BSEP	Basic Skills Education Program
BT	Basic training
CAP III	Centralized Assignment Procedure III System
CE	Commander's evaluation
CHAMPUS	Civilian Health and Medical Program of the Uniformed Services
CID	Criminal Investigation Division
CLEP	College Level Examination Program
CMF	Career management field
COHORT	Cohesion, Operational Readiness, and Training
CONAP	Continental United States area of preference
CONUS	Continental United States
CPMOS	Career progression military occupation specialty
CQ	Charge of quarters
CSEP	Career Soldier's Education Program
CTT	Common Tasks Test
DA	Department of the Army
DANTES	Defense Activity for Non-traditional Education Support
DEERS	Defense Enrollment Eligibility Reporting System
DEROS	Date of estimated return from overseas
DMOS	Duty military occupational specialty
DOD	Department of Defense
DOR	Date of rank
DROS	Date returned from overseas
EAD	Entry on active duty
EER	Enlisted evaluation report
EERWA	Enlisted evaluation report weighted average
EES,	Enlisted Evaluation System
EML	Environmental and morale leave
ENTNAC	Entrance National Agency Check
EOD	Explosive ordnance disposal
EPMS	Enlisted Personnel Management System
ETS	Expiration term of service
FAO	Finance and Accounting Office
FORSCOM	U.S. Army Forces Command
GCM	General Court Martial
GCMCA	General court-martial convening authority

GED	General education development
HAAP	Homebase Advanced Assignment Program
HOR	Home of record
HSDG	High school diploma graduate
IET	Initial entry training
IG	Inspector general
ISR	Individual Soldier's Report
ITEP	Individual Training Program
ITT	Intertheater transfer
JTR	Joint Travel Regulations
JUMPS	Joint Uniform Military Pay Schedule
LES	Leave and Earnings Statement
LOD	Line of duty
MAC	Military Airlift Command
MACOM	Major Army Command
MEDDAC	Medical department activity
MILPERCEN	U.S. Army Military Personnel Center
MILPO	Military personnel office
MPRJ	Military Personnel Records Jacket
MOS	Military Occupational Specialty
NAC	National Agency Check
NCOA	Noncommissioned Officer Academy
NCOES	Noncommissioned Officer Education System
OCONUS	Outside continental United States
OCS	Officer Candidate School
OJE	On-the-job experience
OJT	On-the-job training
OMPF	Official Military Personnel File
OP	Operating procedures
OSUT	One-station unit training
PAC	Personnel and Administration Center
PCS	Permanent change of station
PMOS	Primary military occupational specialty
POR	Preparation of replacements for oversea movement
POV	Privately owned vehicle
PSNCO	Personnel staff noncommissioned officer
PT	Physical training
PTC	Primary technical course
PX	Post exchange
RE code	Reenlistment code
ROTC	Reserve Officers' Training Corps
R&R	Rest and recuperation

SD	Special duty
SDNCO	Staff duty noncommissioned officer
SIDPERS	Standard Installation/Division Personnel Reporting System
SMOS	Secondary military occupational specialty
SOP	Standard operating procedures
SQI	Skill qualification identifier
SQT	Skill qualification test
SRB	Selective reenlistment bonus
SSN	Social security number
TA	Tuition assistance
TCO	Test control officer
TDA	Table of distribution and allowances
TDY	Temporary duty
TE	Technical escort
TIS	Time in service
TOE	Table of organization and equipment
TRADOC	U.S. Army Training and Doctrine Command
TSO	Test Scoring Officer
UCMJ	Uniform Code of Military Justice
USAEREC	U.S. Army Enlisted Records and Evaluation Center
USASSC	U.S. Army Soldier Support Center
USATC	U.S. Army Training Center
USMA	U.S. Military Academy
USMAPS	U.S. Military Academy Preparatory School

Index

Accessories for uniforms, 158, 161, 164
Acting NCO, 96
Additional Skill Identifiers (ASI), 107
Advanced Individual Training (AIT), 34
Advanced Skills Education Program
  (ASEP), 37
Advanced Station Housing Allowances
  (ASHA), 183
Advance leave, 185
Alabama, educational programs in, 53–54
Alaska, educational programs in, 54
Alcohol
  Enlisted Evaluation Report and, 101
  wearing of the uniform and, 18–19
Allowances, monthly, 180
  basic allowance for quarters (BAQ),
    181–82
  basic allowance for subsistence
    (BAS), 181
  clothing maintenance (CMA), 184
  cost-of-living (COLA), 183
  dislocation, 183
  family separation (FSA), 182–83
  per diem, 183–84
  rent-plus, 183
  station housing (SHA), 183
  temporary lodging (TLA), 183
  variable housing (VHA), 183

American College Testing Proficiency
  Examination Program (ACT/PEP), 48
American Council on Education (ACE),
  47–48
American Red Cross, 193
Annual leave, 184–85
Arizona, educational programs in, 54–55
Armed Forces Qualification Test
  (AFQT), 50
Army Apprenticeship Program, 37
Army blue (dress) uniform, 152, 158
Army Board for Correction of Military
  Records, 105
Army College Fund (ACF), 50–51
Army Community Service Center,
  117, 193
Army Continuing Education System
  (ACES), 47
Army Education Centers (AEC), 45–46
Army Emergency Relief (AER) fund, 189,
  192–93
Army green classic service uniform
  (female), 148, 150–51
Army green service uniform (male), 141,
  146–48
Army Natick Research and Development
  Center, 136
Army National Guard, 203–4

Army Physical Fitness Test, 40
Army Reserve Officers' Training Corps
  (ROTC), 203, 208, 210–12
Army Song, The, 26–27
Army Times, 77, 109–10, 175
Army Weight Control Program, 39–40
"At ease" command, 20

Basic Combat Training (BCT), 80
Basic Noncommissioned Officer
  Course, 35
Basic Skills Education Program (BSEP), 37
Basic Training (BT), 34
Battle dress uniforms (BDUs), 137–39
Berets, 158, 161
Board, the, 75–79
  composition of, 76
  dismissal by, 77–78
  dress for, 78
  how to address members of, 77
  NCO of the Month, 76
  reporting to, 76
  responding to, 76–77
  Soldier of the Month, 75, 76
  subject areas for, 79
  See also Promotion board(s)
Bond allotments, 189
Boots, 161
Bugle calls, 24, 26
Buttons, 161

California, educational programs in,
  55–56
Career Management Fields (CMF), 32–34
Chain of Command, 78
  Enlisted, 78–79
Civilian clothing, 135
Civilian salute, 22
Clothing Maintenance Allowance
  (CMA), 184
Coats
  black all-weather, 133, 138
  uniform, 134
Code of Conduct, 15
Cold weather clothing, 136–37, 140–41
College credit by examination, 47–48
College Level Examination Program
  (CLEP), 47
Colorado, educational programs in,
  56–57
Combat arms branch, 33, 34
Combat leader's identification tab, 170

Combat service support branch, 33,
  34, 35
Combat support branch, 33, 34, 35
Combined Federal Campaign (CFC)
  fund, 189
Commander's Evaluation (CE), 83
Commissaries, 191–92
Common Task Test (CTT), 83
Concurrent travel, 118, 119
Convalescent leave, 186
Correspondence courses, 48
Cosmetics, use of, 132
Cost-of-Living Allowances (COLA), 183
Counseling
  Enlisted Evaluation Report and, 97
  nonpromotion and, 88, 93
Courtesies
  to the flag, 22–23, 24
  to officers, 20, 22
Curtailments, overseas travel and, 122

Defense Activity for Nontraditional
  Education Support (DANTES), 47, 48
Deferments, overseas travel and, 121–22
Deferred travel, 118
Deletions, overseas travel and, 121–22
Demolition pay, 178, 180
Desert battle dress uniforms (DBDUs),
  139–40
Diet and nutrition, 40–41
Disapproved travel, 118
Discharges, 199
Dislocation Allowances, 183
Distinctive Unit Insignia (DUI), 170
District of Columbia, educational
  programs in, 57
Diving duty pay, 177
Drill sergeant, 34
Drug abuse, Enlisted Evaluation Report
  and, 101
Dual incentive pay, 180

EDSAV allotments, 189
Educational courses, on-post, 52–71
  See also under name of state
Education requirements for E5/E6
  promotions, minimum, 84
Emergency leave, 185–86
English as a Second Language (ESL)
  courses, 36
Enlisted Chain of Command, 78–79
Enlisted Evaluation Report (EER)
  appeal process, 102–5
  change-of-rater reports, 100

commander inquiry, 102
complete-the-record reports, 100–101
counseling and, 97
purpose of, 96
rating chain, 97
relief-for-cause report, 101
restrictions on information in, 101
special reports and, 100
time limitations and, 97, 100–101
Enlisted Personnel Assignment System,
106–7, 109
Enlisted Personnel Management System
(EPMS), 32
Entering
courtesy to officers entering a room, 20
vehicles by rank, 20
Environmental and Moral Leave (EML)
Program, 186
Europe, educational programs in, 71–72
Evening gun, 23–24
Exercise, 41–42
Experiment stress pay, 180
Extended Cold Weather Clothing System
(ECWCS), 136–37
Eyeglasses
saluting with, 19–20
wearing of, 136

Family Care Plan, 116, 200
Family crisis while overseas, 126
Family Separation Allowance (FSA),
182–83
Federal income taxes, 188
Federal Insurance Contributions Act
(FICA), 188
Federally Insured Student Loan (FISL),
49–50
Females
cosmetics for, 132
haircuts for, 132
handbags for, 138
headgear for, 135, 150–51, 152
knee-length skirts for, 134
overseas travel and pregnant, 120–21
pregnancy options, 199–202
saluting the flag by, 22, 24
slacks for, 134
See also under Uniforms
Financial crisis while overseas, 126
Fingernails, care of, 133
FININ allotments, 189
First call, 24
First Sergeants Course, 35
Flag
civilian salute to the, 22

courtesy to the, 22–23, 24
dipping of the, 22
at half-staff, 23
raising and lowering of the, 23, 24
saluting the, 20, 22, 24
sizes for the, 22–23
terms associated with the, 23
Flight pay, 178
Foreign duty pay, 176–77

Garrison flag, 22
Georgia, educational programs in, 57–58
GI Bill, new, 51–52
Gloves
with battle dress uniforms, 138
with cold weather uniforms, 140–41
with desert battle dress uniforms, 140
Graduation leave, 186
Grants, educational, 49
Grave decorating flag, 23
Green maternity service uniform, 152
Grooming
cosmetics, 132
facial hair, 132
fingernails, 133
haircuts, 131–32
Guaranteed Student Loan (GSL), 49–50
Guidance and counseling, 47

Haircuts, 131–32
Handbags, use of, 138
Hand salute, 19, 22
Hawaii, educational programs in, 59–60
Hazardous Duty Incentive Pay (HDIP),
178
Headgear, 135
with Army green classic service
uniforms (female), 150–51
with Army green service uniforms
(male), 146
with battle dress uniforms, 138
berets, 158, 161
with cold weather uniforms, 140
with desert battle dress uniforms, 139
with green maternity service
uniforms, 152
rain cap covers, 161
saluting when wearing, 20
Headquarters, Department of the Army
(HQDA), 82
HOME allotments, 189
Homebase and Advance Assignment
Program (HAAP), 124
Hostile fire pay, 177

Housing allowance. *See* Allowances, monthly

Illinois, educational programs in, 60
Indiana, educational programs in, 61
Indoors, saluting, 20
Initial Entry Training (IET), 32, 34–35
INS allotments, 189
Insignia
  branch, 164
  combat leader's identification tab, 170
  distinctive unit (DUI), 170
  of grade, 164
  nameplates, 170
  ribbons and medals, 170–73
  shoulder marks, 164
  shoulder sleeve (SSI), 164, 170
Intelligence Course, 35

Jackets, uniform, 134
Japan/Okinawa, educational programs in, 72
Jewelry, wearing of, 136
Joint Domicile Program, 111
Judge Advocate General's (JAG) Corps, 195

Kansas, educational programs in, 61
Kentucky, educational programs in, 61–62

Leave
  advance, 185
  annual, 184-85
  convalescent, 186
  emergency, 185–86
  Environmental and Moral Leave Program, 186
  graduation, 186
  rest and recuperation (R&R), 186
  special, 186
Leave and Earnings Statement (LES), 174–75
Legal assistance, 194–97
Loans, educational, 49
  repayment program, 49–50
Louisiana, educational programs in, 62

Married Army Couples (MAC) Program, 110, 111
Marsh, John O., Jr., 45

Maryland, educational programs in, 62–63
Massachusetts, educational programs in, 63–64
Maternity work uniform, 139
  green maternity service uniform, 152
MBOND allotments, 189
Medals, wearing of, 170–73
  U.S. military decorations, 171–72
  U.S. service medals, 173
  U.S. unit awards, 172
Medical care/medications, overseas travel and, 125–26
Michigan, educational programs in, 64
Military Personnel Center (MILPERCEN), 107
  Personnel Assistance Point (PAP), 125
Military Personnel Offices (MILPOs), 86, 107
Military police, 34
  clothing for, 137
Missouri, educational programs in, 64
MOSs, 32, 46
  Related Instruction courses, 37
  training of, 34

Nameplates, 170
National Anthem, 24
National anthems of other countries, 24
National color, 23
National Defense Student Loan, 49–50
National ensign, 23
National standard, 23
New Jersey, educational programs in, 64–65
New Mexico, educational programs in, 65
New York, educational programs in, 65–66
Noncommissioned Officers Academies (NCOA), 35
Noncommissioned Officer Education System (NCOES), 30, 32, 35, 37, 83
Noncommissioned Officer of the Month, 76
Nonpromotable status, 94–96
North Carolina, educational programs in, 66

Officer Candidate School (OCS), 204
Officers, courtesies to, 20, 22
Oklahoma, educational programs in, 66–67
One Station Unit Training (OSUT), 80
Overseas extension pay, 178

Overseas Orientation Program, 112
Overseas schooling, 71–74
Overseas theaters, transfers in, 123–24
Overseas travel. *See* Travel, overseas

Panama, educational programs in, 72–73
Parachute duty pay, 178
Passes, 187
Passports, overseas travel and, 124
Patton, George S., Jr., 17, 18
Pay
  advance, 187–88
  basic pay table, 175
  deductions from, 188-90
  demolition, 178, 180
  diving duty, 177
  dual incentive, 180
  experiment stress, 180
  flight, 178
  foreign duty, 176–77
  Hazardous Duty Incentive, 178
  hostile fire, 177
  how paychecks can be disbursed, 175
  Leave and Earnings Statement, 174–75
  monthly allowances, 180–84
  monthly pay entitlements, 176–78, 180
  once or twice a month payments, 175
  overseas extension, 178
  parachute duty, 178
  reenlistment bonuses, 184
  sea duty, 177
  special duty assignment, 176
  toxic fuels/propellants, 180
Pennsylvania, educational programs
    in, 67
Per diem allowances, 183–84
Personnel and administration center
    (PAC), 86
Physical fitness training, 37–42, 44
  diet and nutrition, 40–41
  exercise, 41–42
  tests, 42, 44
  weight control, 38–40
Physical qualifications, promotions
    and, 84
Pledge of Allegiance, 23
Post flag, 22
Pregnant soldiers
  options for, 199–202
  overseas travel and, 120–21
  weight control and, 40, 120-21
Primary Leadership Development Course,
    (PLDC), 30, 35
Primary Technical Courses (PTC), 35
Promotion board(s), 85–86, 88, 93–94

composition of, 85
point system used by, 86, 88
recorder on a, 85–86
Promotions, 79–86, 88, 93–96
  Acting NCO and, 96
  to E2, 80
  to E3, 81
  to E4, 81–82
  to E5 and E6, 82–83, 84–85
  Enlisted Evaluation Report and, 96–97,
    100–105
  nonpromotable status, 94–96
  physical qualifications for, 84
  reasons for disqualification, 84
  reevaluation and recomputation of
    points, 93–94
  required counseling, 88, 93
  security clearances and, 84
  service-remaining obligation and,
    84–85
  Skill Qualification Test and, 81, 83–84
  under unusual circumstances, 94
  waivers and, 82, 84
Public Law, 98–525, 51
Puerto Rico, educational programs in, 73

Rain cap covers, 161
Reagan, Ronald, 37–38
REDCR allotments, 189
Reenlisting, 204, 206–8
Reenlistment bonuses, 184, 202–3
Relief agencies, 192–93
Rent-plus allowance, 183
Report for Suspension of Favorable
    Personnel Actions, 95–96
Reserves, 203
Rest and recuperation (R&R), 186
Retreat
  the flag and, 23
  purpose of retreat ceremony, 23
  showing of respect during, 24
Reveille, 23
Ribbons and medals, 170–73
ROTC, 208, 210–12
Rucksack, wearing of, 134
Running and saluting, 19

Salute, the, 19–20
  civilian salute, 22
  indoors and, 20
Saluting the flag, 20, 22, 24
Scarves, 161
Scholarships, 49
Sea duty pay, 177
Security clearances, promotions and, 84

Selective Reenlistment Bonus (SRB), 202–3
Servicemembers' Opportunity Colleges (SOC), 46, 52
Servicemembers' Opportunity Colleges Associate Degree (SOCAD), 52–53
Servicemen's Group Life Insurance (SGLI), 188
Shoulder marks, 164
Shoulder sleeve insignia (SSI), 164, 170
Skill Qualification Identifiers (SQI), 107
Skill Qualification Test (SQT), 81, 83–84
Skirts, knee-length, 134
Slacks, for females, 134
Soldier of the Month boards, 75, 76
Soldiers' and Sailors' Civil Relief Act (SSCRA), 196–97
"Soldier's Creed, The," 27, 29
Soldier's Manual of Common Tasks, 76
South Carolina, educational programs in, 67
South Korea, educational programs in, 74
Space-available travel, 194
Special Clothing Allowance (SCA), 184
Special duty assignment pay, 176
Special Services, 194
Sponsorship programs, 112, 117, 124
SPT-V allotments, 189
Standing at attention, 22, 24
State income taxes, 188
Station Housing Allowances (SHA), 183
Storm flag, 22–23
Subject Standardized Test (DSST), 47
Sweaters, 161

Taps, 26
Tattoo, 26
Temporary Lodging Allowances (TLA), 183
Texas, educational programs in, 67–68
To the Color, 24, 26
Toxic fuels/propellants pay, 180
Travel, overseas, 107, 109, 110–28
    concurrent, 118, 119
    deferments, deletions, and curtailments, 121–22
    deferred, 118
    disapproved, 118
    documents needed for, 124
    Environmental and Moral Leave (EML) Program, 186
    family crisis while, 126
    financial crisis while, 126
    Homebase and Advance Assignment Program, 124
    length of service, 112–16

lost airline ticket while, 126
lost baggage while, 127
lost/stolen documents while, 127
for married couples, 110–11, 118
medical care/medications and, 125–26
Overseas Orientation Program, 112
passports and, 124
pregnant servicewomen and, 120–121
privately owned vehicles and, 119
role of the soldier while, 127-28
soldiers with dependents and, 116–19
soldiers with no dependents and, 119–20
sponsorship programs, 112, 117, 124
volunteering, 122–24
Travel benefits, 194
Travelope, 124–25
Travel within the United States
    assignments for married couples, 110–12
    Enlisted Personnel Assignment System, 106–7, 109
    exchanging assignments, 109–10
    requests for early arrival, 107
Trousers, 134
Tuition assistance, 48–49

Umbrellas, use of, 19
Undergarments, 134
Uniforms
    accessories for, 158, 161, 164
    appearance and fit, 133–34
    Army blue (dress), 152, 158
    Army green classic service (female), 148, 150–51
    Army green service (male), 141, 146-48
    battle dress, 137–39
    changes in, 136–37
    Class A, 135
    Class B, 135
    cold weather, 140–41
    desert battle dress, 139–40
    green maternity service, 152
    insignia on, 164, 170–73
    maternity work, 139
    physical fitness, 137
    religious exceptions to, 131
    when to wear, 134–36
    See also under type of clothing
United Code of Military Justice (UCMJ), 195–96
U.S. Army Sergeants Major Academy (USASMA), 35
U.S. Military Academy at West Point, 206

U.S. Military Academy Preparatory School
   (USMAPS), 206–8
U.S. military decorations, 171–72
U.S. service medals, 173
United States Soldier's Home (USSH), 188
U.S unit awards, 172
USA Today, 77
USO, 193
Utah, educational programs in, 68

Variable Housing Allowances (VHA), 183
Vehicles
   entering by rank, 20
   overseas travel and privately owned, 119
   position of subordinates in, 20

retreat ceremony and, 24
saluting passing military, 20
Veterans Educational Assistance Program
   (VEAP), 50–51, 190
Virginia, educational programs in, 68–70

Waivers, promotions and, 82, 84
Walking, position of subordinates
   when, 20
Warrant Officer Flight Training (WOFT),
   204, 206
Washington, educational programs in, 71
Washington, George, 17
Weight control, 38–40
Windbreakers, 161, 164

Some other fine military and gun books from Stackpole
Your Military Publisher for Over 50 Years

Roots of Strategy
The 5 greatest military classics of all time—complete in one volume
edited by Brig. Gen. T. R. Phillips

Guide to Effective Military Writing
A Handbook for Getting Things Written Quickly, Correctly, and Easily
by William A. McIntosh

Transition from Military to Civilian Life
How to Plan a Bright Future <u>Now</u> for You and Your Family
by James D. Canfield and Merle Dethlefsen

The Guide to Military Installations
A comprehensive guide to the location, facilities, housing, climate, and customs of all Army, Navy, Air Force, and Marine installations in the U.S. and overseas
by Dan Cragg

Combat Leader's Field Guide
Information for the combat leader in a handy, pocket-sized volume

The Army Officer's Guide: 43rd Edition
The single, immediate reference for well over one million officers and aspiring officers
by Lt. Col. Lawrence P. Crocker, USA (Ret.)

The NCO Guide: 2nd Edition
Provides the noncommissioned officer of the eighties with guidelines for every official and social situation
by Sgt. Maj. Dan Cragg, USA (Ret.)

The Air Force Officer's Guide: 27th Edition
Up-to-date techniques for career advancement direct from the most knowledgeable military sources
by Lt. Col. John Hawkins Napier III, USA (Ret.)

Parent's Guide to the 5 U.S. Service Academies
A Firsthand Personal Account of What You Can Expect Along the Way
by Helen Powers

The AK47 Story
Evolution of the Kalashnikov Weapons
by Edward Clinton Ezell

Beretta Automatic Pistols
The Collector's and Shooter's Comprehensive Guide
by J. B. Wood

Small Arms Today
Latest Reports on the World's Weapons and Ammunition
by Edward Clinton Ezell

Available at your local bookstore, or for complete ordering information, write:
Stackpole Books
Dept. ESG
Cameron and Kelker Streets
Harrisburg, PA 17105
For fast service credit card users may call 1-800-READ-NOW
In Pennsylvania, call 717-234-5041